P9-DXJ-676

HOUSEBOAT

on the

SEINE

Also by William Wharton

BIRDY
DAD*
A MIDNIGHT CLEAR*
SCUMBLER*
PRIDE*
TIDINGS
FRANKY FURBO
LAST LOVERS
EVER AFTER*

* Published by Newmarket Press

HOUSEBOAT
on the
SEINE

WILLIAM WHARTON

NEWMARKET PRESS

Copyright © 1996 by William Wharton

This book is published in the United States of America.

All rights reserved. This book may not be reproduced, in whole,
or in part, in any form, without written permission.
Inquiries should be addressed to Permissions Department,
Newmarket Press, 18 East 48th Street, New York 10017.

96 97 98 99 10 9 8 7 6 5 4 3 2 1

Library of Congress Cataloging-in-Publication Data
Wharton, William.
    Houseboat on the Seine / William Wharton.
        p.   cm.
    ISBN 1-55704-272-1
    1. Wharton, William—Homes and haunts—France—Le Port-Marly.
2. Houseboats—France—Le Port-Marly. 3. Boat living—France—Le Port-
Marly.   I. Title.
DC801.L586W48   1996
643'.2—dc20   95-49330
                                                                                CIP

Quantity Purchases
Companies, professional groups, clubs, and other organizations
may qualify for special terms when ordering five or more copies.
For information contact: Special Sales, Newmarket Press,
18 East 48th Street, New York, N.Y. 10017, or call (212) 832-3575.

Text design by Tina Thompson.
Manufactured in the United States of America.

To the river we love and all who live on it.

"Love this river, stay by it, learn from it." Yes, he wanted to learn from it, he wanted to listen to it. It seemed to him that whoever understood this river and its secrets, would understand much more, many secrets, all secrets.

—HERMANN HESSE
Siddhartha

HOUSEBOAT
on the
SEINE

CHAPTER I

Kindergarten Entrapment

MY WIFE, ROSEMARY, was for twenty-five years a kindergarten teacher at the American School of Paris. Last year, by French law, she was forced to retire. I must say, almost everything I've ever really needed to know, I learned from my kindergarten-teaching wife, except somehow, she never taught me how to live on a houseboat.

About twenty-five years ago, she worked with a lovely woman named Pauline Lee. Pauline taught first grade next to Rosemary, and lived on the Seine in a houseboat. The houseboat was located in the small village of Le Port Marly, not far from Versailles and St. Germain-en-Laye, ten miles west of Paris proper.

One day, Pauline suggested that the kindergarten and the first grade go out on a field trip to visit her houseboat.

My wife was enchanted with what she saw. I don't really know if the kindergarten children were—that's not my concern. My main concern is my wife, and she's something to be concerned about. Anyway, she came home all excited and wanting to live on a house-boat. That sounded crazy enough, but was OK with me. Rosemary is subject to these impulsive, out-of-this-world decisions, and I've learned to go along for the ride.

"Just tell Pauline to keep an eye out in case there are any cheap boats available, dear."

I'd had a few good painting sales for a change, and was feeling relatively flush. Oh, how easily one can dive in over one's head . . . literally! My problem was I didn't actually believe any of this was for real.

Three weeks later, Pauline calls to tell us a houseboat only four boats toward Paris from theirs had burned to the waterline over New Year's Eve, and she thought it might be for sale. We contact the owners, and sure enough it is. And I might say, *for good reason,* more good reasons than I could possibly realize.

That weekend, we drive out to look at this boat. It's a beautiful day, and I'm thinking that maybe we can take a nice walk in the forest at St.-Germain-en-Laye. We stop by Pauline's, and she points out the boat that's for sale.

We thought we would be having Pauline as a neighbor, but it didn't work out that way. Bob, her husband, had been very much involved with the students during what the French call "Les Événements de Mai," that is the Student Revolution. When all the smoke died down, Bob was asked to leave by the administration of the school where he worked, The American College of Paris. He not only left the job, but he and his wife left the country as well. They went back to Michigan, where Pauline is again teaching.

We look over the quay down a muddy hill to the water. This is a flat-bottomed wooden boat, sixteen feet wide by fifty-four feet long. It's actually more like a house than a boat. It has no real bow or stern. It's just rectangular and flat. There's no motor, no sails. It has wood siding with windows, the kind you might find in any ordinary house. It even has shutters on the windows. I'm thinking, where are the portholes? Pauline explains this boat had been built on an old sand barge by a French Arctic explorer named Victor Émile, sort of a French version of Admiral Peary, for his lady friend. That sounds romantic enough, but this boat isn't very romantic now.

Pauline has the key, so we walk down the squishy quay on

stone steps, then up a small gangplank and into the boat. It's completely smoke-damaged, the ceiling's burned out with bare electrical wires hanging everywhere, and most shockingly impressive . . . truly burned down to the water on the river side. The water laps into the boat when scullers swish by. These turn out to be the main traffic on this dead arm of the Seine where the boat is located. There are about a dozen or so houseboats in this area, protected by an island in the center of the river. The advantage is the houseboats do not bounce with the backwash of each huge barge as it hauls cargo from Le Havre to Paris and back.

Pauline explains all this with verve and enthusiasm. I just want to hop back in our car and go for a walk in the forest. But our children are as enchanted as my wife. Now, *this* would be exciting living, not the way it is in dirty old Paris. Can you believe it? I swear, this damned boat is bewitching, or maybe our children are getting too *blasé!*

"Smell the air, Dad, how great it would be to live out here after all the pollution in Paris."

I sniff. It smells like an open sewer to me. This was over twenty-five years ago, and at that time, the Seine *was* virtually an open sewer. Paris and all the villages along the river down from Paris, in a beautiful, long, meandering curve, were dumping raw sewage directly into the river. Naturally, this boat is *down*river from Paris!

To make everybody, that is, wife and kids, happy, I put in a ridiculous, insulting bid for this crippled wooden hulk. We go for our walk, and I'm ready to forget about the whole thing.

A week later, I'm shocked when my bid is accepted. Accept is mild—they jump at it. Yet, little as I bid, I must borrow money to swing this cockeyed, insane deal. Painters are rarely rich, or even reasonably comfortable. I often challenge friends to name fifty American painters making a regular living painting—not teaching, or working in TV or films, or in advertising—just painting pictures and selling them. Sometimes, there will be a flurry for a particular painter, but it rarely lasts more than a few years, then it's back to the old easel and bean soup, especially if a painter happens to have a family. No one has ever come up with more than twenty who are truly making it. But it is a great life. So it goes.

For the next three months, my painting is suspended in the interest of romance, excitement, adventure, WITCHCRAFT—such an important change for a man who lives in the streets or out in fields and likes it. I'm feeling caught up in something wicked. I am! I'm not a river man. The Seine, for me, is something to paint. It is constantly moving, changing, at the same time it is still, like a good model.

Our lives up to this point have been something of a dream. I was an art teacher in the Los Angeles City Schools until 1960. Then, since I saw myself as an artist, not a teacher, we came to Europe. One of the main reasons was to keep our children away from American television. Also, at that time, living was cheaper here.

First we lived in a very small apartment in Paris, three hundred square feet, which we bought with my retirement money from the Los Angeles schools. We were very mobile, Paris in spring and fall, Bavaria in summer and for Christmas, then southern Spain for winter. It sounds like a millionaire's life, but we were doing all this on three hundred dollars a month, plus my disability pension from World War II. Yes, if you're careful, it can be done. For us, the poverty line is way above our heads.

When we had three children, we moved into an old carpenter's workshop that we fixed up as an apartment. When I say *"we,"* I mean anyone in the family who could swing a hammer or spread paint with a brush. It was something like the boat project, mostly a family affair.

CHAPTER II

A Brief Enchantment

FIRST, I BUILD up that side with the water sloshing in. Then I clean out and scrape or scrap all the charred interior. This involves, among other things, replacing forty-five small mullioned window-panes. There are also two huge plate-glass view windows that are so smoke- and soot-covered, nothing can be seen through them—two more days of scrubbing there. The walls of what served as a living room and bedroom are beyond mere painting; they will take more serious treatment.

I find a bolt of gold brocade cloth at the Marché Aligré, a street market near our apartment-cum-studio in Paris. For some reason, this brocade is only about the price of burlap, so I buy it all, three bolts full. I begin to know I'm going crazy because I look forward to sticking this cloth over all the black walls and ceilings. I'm being carried away. Perhaps the entire boat is enchanted.

I use paste to cover the walls and ceiling so I can attach the gold brocade—it does cover a multitude of sins. I buy inexpensive light fixtures with amber lightbulbs, and, after some considerable electrical work, much beyond my skill level, manage to fix them so they actually light, even turn on and off with primitive switches.

I call in the rest of the family on weekends to scrub out the bathroom, the kitchen, the usual comfort necessities. These are all a uniform smoke-brownish hue. Before the school year ends, late in June, we have the boat finished. According to my wife, it looks like a drunken pirate's private whorehouse—she's very conservative in these kinds of things.

The layout of the houseboat is quite simple. After one comes up the gangplank, one goes through a low oaken door, about five-feet six-inches high. I'm five-foot-ten. After bumping my head the tenth time, I consider wearing a hard hat permanently, or maybe an old-time bowler.

The door opens onto a tiny vestibule. Turning right, one goes through two swinging mahogany doors with beautiful brass fittings, very boatlike. These doors lead down two steps into the main room. On the left, looking out over the river, now, after much scraping, is one of two large plate windows. It's about seven feet wide and four feet high.

The living room is approximately twenty feet long and fifteen feet wide. At the far end, on the river side, is an entry to a small kitchen. In the center of that end wall is another pair of mahogany doors like those opening from the vestibule. These doors lead to a narrow hall with a bathroom, complete with toilet, sink and shower, opening on the right, the shore side.

Directly ahead are three steps up to the bedroom. Here we find the second of the large plate windows, also looking out on the river.

All along the shore side are small windows, four in all, opening onto the quay. These are house-type windows with shutters. There is also a window of the same design opening onto the kitchen on the river side.

It must have been a lovely place for the French explorer and his lady friend. I'm not sure how it's going to work with a family of five, though.

We rent the boat out for the summer to a young woman

(another witch) who works for the Foire de Trône, a sort of yearly carnival in Le Bois de Vincennes. My contract for our boat location stipulates someone must be on the boat at all times. The river-navigation people are already very suspicious of this crippled craft.

We leave for our usual summer vacation to the old water mill we'd bought in Burgundy when we first came to France. We paid the huge sum of two thousand dollars for this place. It was another romantic *coup de foudre.* Actually, the mill is only a three-hundred-year-old stone tent, but that's another story.

Disenchantment!

We hadn't been at the mill three weeks when we receive a telegram, our first French telegram. It's from an elderly English couple who live two boats downriver from us. I don't know why they wrote it in French. It says:

Votre bateau a coulé.

That's said coo-lay, as in Kool-Aid.

I run across the street to a French neighbor hoping to find out what the word "coulé" means. As if I didn't know! I just don't want to believe it.

I immediately take the train up to Paris, then the bus out to where the boat is. It is, indeed, *coulé.* Only a small corner of the roof is sticking above water. There is a medium-sized crowd along the bank. They surround the boat, babbling in French. Each seems to have a different idea as to why the boat has sunk. All of them, in French fashion, are convinced there must be a reason, *C'est logique, n'est-ce pas?*

After much running around, trying to find someone to lift the boat out of the water and getting nowhere, someone tells me about specialists in this kind of work, bringing up sunken boats. They are called *les frères Teurnier.* I phone them from the café on the corner.

This town of Le Port Marly has seven restaurants, but only one café. It's directly across the street from the *boule* courts, which are on the *chemin de halage,* or path, next to our boat. There are also two *restaurants de routiers,* sort of truck stops that double as cafés.

The next day, a broken down old *"deux chevaux"* pulls up on the *chemin de halage* beside the boat. I'd camped, somewhat chillily, on *la berge* overnight. The man who climbs out of this car is in his sixties and about five feet tall. He's wearing French workmen's blues, filthy, stiff with oil and sweat, and a mariner's cap, also filthy.

He shakes my hand, jabbers away, smiles, then pulls down a plank from the top of his car. He slides down the steep riverbank and throws the plank out across the water, between the land and the projecting bit of boat roof. I'm convinced he's going to sink the whole business, but he walks like an acrobat, muttering to himself, out on that board. After looking down all sides of the boat, seeing I can't imagine what, except dirty, black water, he comes back to me and, in a complex mixture of Breton, French, my broken French and his violent pantomime, I come to know he thinks he can raise the boat for two thousand francs (at that time about four hundred dollars).

This represents the amount we still owe on the boat and were hoping to pay off in September. I actually have it in my pocket in one-hundred-franc bills, twenty of them, plus some change. At the moment, it represents virtually our total capital.

In French and in pantomime again, he tells me he will wrap the boat with a large cloth, then pump the water out so the boat can come to the surface and we can see what's wrong. It sounds crazy. However, he insists that before he can put the pumps in the boat to pump out the water, I must go down inside and remove anything floating in there. If I don't, they'll jam his pumps.

With this advice, he leaves, promising he'll be back in three days to commence the rescue operation.

———

Losing My Suntan

I look at the boat. It's noon, the bells of the village church are ring-
ing. I figure I might as well start right off. Luckily, the crowds have
diminished. In the bright sunlight, I strip down to my Jockey
shorts and slide into the water. Happily, as a last-minute decision,
I've also brought along from the mill a waterproof flashlight, a
Christmas present for Matt, our fifteen-year-old son.

Usually we leave the key right in the boat door. When I'm feeling around in the blackness of water, holding my breath, I find the
key. Our renter must have left it there, too. I'm half afraid to go in,
expecting she might still be inside, floating, bloated, in our living
room.

I turn the key and the door opens sluggishly. I come up inside
and there *is* an air pocket. M. Teurnier had said there probably
would be. I take a deep, ghoulish breath and look around. It's dark
and things are floating around as he expected, but no bodies, yet.
I flash the light around the dark interior. My God, the place is
filled with junk: floating doors, cabinet doors, real doors; pillows,
mattresses, papers, furniture, bits of furniture; all floating in the
dark. Also, there are other things floating, things I hadn't expected,
though I should have. I strap the flashlight to my head with a torn
piece of wet sheet and get started.

I spend the rest of that day pulling out the floaters and spreading them on the bank. Chairs, tables, anything held together with
glue, are no longer in one piece. I fish away, in and out, down and
up, until dark settles over all and fatigue drags me to the ground.

Just before the bakery closes, I buy a baguette for dinner. I sit
on the *berge* and watch the sun go down behind me. The tempta-
tion is strong just to walk away and allow someone else to deal
with this mess, write it all off.

The evening is warm. I curl up and fall asleep. But I wake in
the middle of the night with severe stomach cramps. My baguette

goes out the way it went in and, simultaneously, the way it *should* come out. I accompany these gratuitous acts of my body with much grunting, groaning and feeble whining.

When the morning finally comes, I put on some clothes and walk across to the Café Brazza, the same one Alfred Sisley painted several times when the river was in full flood. I'll never look at those paintings the same way, beautiful as they are. I use the café phone to contact a farmhouse with the only phone near our mill. They'll pass on a message to my family that I'm all right, but I'll be staying up here awhile, trying to raise the boat. It sounds so simple. I give the message on the edge of tears, tears of self-pity.

Back on the *berge,* I start my diving again. I'm now having the heaves out both ends. I didn't know this was possible. There's nothing in there anyway, and the river wouldn't mind if there were. I'm as polluted as *it* is.

I don't eat lunch. It seems like suicide, and, as I said, I'm very short on money. Who'd pay for the funeral? Then I notice that my skin is peeling off in great slabs. I'm baby pink underneath. My beginning summer tan is turning a gray-black and slipping away. It falls off my head and face and droops like a veil over my beard. I feel miserable, shaking inside and trembling outside. But I am pulling the last floating things from the boat. After that, I'll have a day or two of rest. I'm having blackout spells. Time mysteriously passes, and I find myself on the ground. For some reason, it doesn't seem serious to me, that's how far gone I am.

The Royal Mounted Police Arrive

The next part of this tale I didn't experience directly. I was told about it ten years later under unusual circumstances.

A Canadian-American family had rented a boat downriver, the same boat Pauline and Bob had rented. They were walking their five children along the *chemin de halage.* This is a dirt road beside the river, which, in the old days, was used for horses and mules to pull the barges up to the locks in Bougival. The barges were much smaller in those times.

This family, out for a walk, looks over the edge of the *berge* and sees me, virtually naked, curled in the fetal position and moaning. The children insist their parents check to see what's the matter.

They're shocked when I look up at them, or at least seem to, and speak English, American English. I don't remember a thing, not what I said, none of it. The entire family, all seven of them, drag me down to their boat, actually carrying me part of the way. They put my heaving hulk into a bunk bed and try forcing food into me. Carol, the wife, pats cold cream over the bare red patches of my body.

They're sure I'd just managed to survive from the sinking boat they've seen in the water behind me. I remember none of this, either.

I stay with these kindly people on their boat that night and the next day. But, on the third day, I'm conscious enough to explain the situation, how M. Teurnier will be coming to raise my boat and will be needing me.

I force my way onto my feet groggily and stagger back to the *chemin de halage,* thence to the *berge* with the sunken barge. M. Teurnier and another man are already there. They have a truck pulling a small boat on a trailer. They stare at me. My basic French isn't enough. Don, the Canadian husband and father of the family, has come with me. He's afraid I'll collapse. He speaks French well —at least it sounds good to me. This part I can vaguely remember.

It turns out the river here is filled with sulfuric acid dumped at the Renault automobile plant upriver. M. Teurnier had assumed I knew this and so would be using a wet suit when I went into the river. He and the other man both look surprised that I'm alive. I know I must look like Lazarus risen from the grave with my gray skin flapping in pieces like a rotted grave shroud around me.

They go to work immediately, Don helping where he can, while I stumble weakly around trying to be of some assistance. They nail a large canvas tarpaulin all around the roof of the boat, letting it float down with weights along the sides. Then they set up a humongous pump and begin pumping. Water spurts out of a six-inch-diameter exit pipe. It shoots up into the air and splashes down into the river with a tumultuous, continuous crashing noise. A crowd has gathered again to watch the excitement. In the mêlée, I can't find Don. Later, I discover this was the day they were scheduled to depart, and despite the complaints of their children, he couldn't stay. I've lost my translator and trusty worker, and don't see him again for twenty years.

The pump spouts water continually, but the boat, despite all this feverish activity, rises only a few inches, then settles back on the bottom, not unlike a beached, dying whale I once saw in California. They turn off the pump. I understand M. Teurnier saying to his brother that it must be a huge hole. They set up a second pump with an exit spout twice the size of the first. They turn this one on, and, with the two going, the boat makes a tremendous effort. The pumps make a horrendous racket, but the boat rises only slightly, then with what appears an overwhelming fatigue, settles back to the bottom. I'm weak and feeling much the same as the feelings I project into the boat.

Les Scaphandriers

Next, M. Teurnier begins to dress in a genuine diver's outfit, a heavy canvas suit with oxygen tanks to feed a brass helmet over his head and face. He walks into the water, wearing weights around his neck, checks his hoses, pauses as his brother screws the helmet onto the top of the suit and clamps it. M. Teurnier signals with one finger to start the oxygen flowing and walks down and in, I presume through the same door I've been slogging in and out of during the few days I could work.

He comes back to the surface every fifteen minutes or so and tells us with hand signals and head shaking that he's found nothing, no hole. He gives the signal to start the smaller of the two pumps. Water is rushing out again. This time, after only about five minutes, he comes staggering up the slippery bank clasping something in his left hand. His brother turns off the pump and opens the helmet.

M. Teurnier pushes his hand in front of my face, stares at me with his violet-blue eyes.

"On vous a bien eu."

I don't know what this means any more than *coulé*. A young woman on the bank shouts to me in British English. I listen hard after all the noise.

"Monsieur, he says you have been had!"

I also keep hearing another word that sounds like *scaf on drier* or maybe that's several words run together. I look up at her.

"Monsieur, don't you realize how lucky you are? They are *scaphandriers* and the work is very dangerous."

I look down at M. Teurnier. He seems to be embarrassed. I feel the rotted wood in his gloved hand. It's like sponge. Maybe this is lucky, but it doesn't seem like that to me. M. Teurnier undresses from his diving costume, stands briefly, shivering in his briefs, and dresses in his work clothes again. We walk across the street for a beer. I invite the young woman to join us. She's somewhat leery, and I don't blame her. I beg her to translate, she agrees and I order her a beer.

She's all excited, it's as bad as Rosemary with this damned boat when she first saw it. She babbles on in English.

"These men are called *les pieds-lourds* because of the heavy leaded shoes they wear. This *équipe* that's working on your boat is famous. Originally, it was a father and his sons. The father started as a *scaphandrier* in 1912; they specialize in *renflouage,* that is, bringing up sunken boats such as yours. You should be very proud."

I don't want to hear any more. This woman must be mad. I stare at her.

"How do you know all this? It seems like very specialized knowledge, especially for a young Englishwoman like you."

She smiles at me.

"I am a student at *l'École des mines.* Also, I have always had a special interest in underwater work. A friend of mine told me about your boat sinking, and I came here to watch."

Over the beer, M. Teurnier explains through the young woman that there is at least one completely rotten plank going from one side of the boat to the other. This is what blew out and caused the boat to sink.

"But is it possible to bring it up again?"

His answer translates into the idea of shoving some large sheets of plywood under the suspect section, pumping to see if the boat will come up, then inspecting the damage.

The Surfacing Whale

So, that's what we do. M. Teurnier dresses again in his diving costume, forces pieces of plywood under the leaking sections, then gives the signal for the pumps to start.

This time the boat starts rising and keeps on rising. Again it's like a huge whale surfacing, only alive and well, more or less well. There are shouts of encouragement and applause from the village people along the bank. M. Teurnier stays down, manipulating the plywood until the hole or holes in the hull are covered. Within half an hour, the boat, filthy, waterlogged, has surfaced. M. Teurnier opens the only door to the cabin fully, and the last of the water flows out. I walk over the slippery gangplank and go inside. The entire interior is covered with dark brown mud, the consistency of thick *crème fraîche,* or nonemulsified peanut butter.

Again, like a latter-day astronaut, he's undressed by his brother and jumps into his regular French blues. We go back to the café. The young woman who has been translating and instructing me as to the mysteries of *les scaphandriers* says she has a class and must leave. I try paying for her help with nonexistent money, but, thankfully, she'll take nothing, which is about what I have to offer. She wishes me good luck and *bon courage.* Good luck, courage and more is what I need, all right.

We eat lunch at the nearest *routier. Les frères Teurnier* discuss what can be done. After a full bottle of wine and steaks with *frites,* we drive in the truck to a building-supply house. M. Teurnier buys five sacks of premixed, quick-drying, anhydrous concrete. We drive back to the scene of the crime, remove the rotted parts of the guilty board and pour the concrete over the entire area, mixing it with river water. We keep building small dams to hold the concrete in place over the damaged sections. We watch to see if the water will seep through or around it. M. Teurnier keeps looking out one of the mud-smeared windows. Everyone, except me, lights up cigarettes. Then he points out the window. One of the plywood pieces is floating away. He pulls it in with a grappling hood, then manages to hook the other as it too loosens. He's smiling. Finally, I understand what's happening. Now there's no longer the pressure of water onto the boat holding the boards against the hull, so it means the leak is effectively stopped—more or less, that is.

We smile all around, a bottle of wine is brought out from the back of the truck and they somehow manage to open it with a bent nail. I don't know what to do next. M. Teurnier takes his slug at the bottle and passes it on.

He pulls me along with him to the boat just next to mine, downriver. He rings a bell hanging on the door, till somebody comes. It's a very dignified-looking Frenchman. M. Teurnier rattles away in his Breton French. The man looks at me and speaks in French-accented, but clear, English.

"I always knew that boat would sink someday, wooden bottom and no one taking care of it. You must remember, monsieur, you have bought a boat with a house on it, not a house with a boat under it. There is a big difference."

So I'm not ready for more lectures. M. Teurnier explains the problem, I can see from his pantomime. He does it even when he's speaking French to another Frenchman. He looks at me. The man, whose name is M. Le Clerc, looks at me. He shrugs and then concentrates.

"I do not believe any *chantier,* I mean slip, around here would take a noncommercial ship with a wooden *coque* for repairs. You could have a *sabot,* a metal shoe, made and slipped under your boat, but that would be very expensive. I do not really know, monsieur. Perhaps it is best to accept the loss and have the boat destroyed. It will be nothing but *souci,* trouble, otherwise."

His wife comes out with some cold white wine and frosted glasses on a tray with white napkins. She offers the tray around. I think of the bottle of red we've just slurped down, each wiping his lips on mud-encrusted sleeves of "blues," after drinking. Contrast, the punctuation of life.

When we finish, M. Le Clerc gives us a slight bow of dismissal, his lovely, tall wife smiles and we leave. His boat is really a masterpiece of how one can live in style on the Seine. I look back. It lies low in the water, and the upper floor has amber translucent windowpanes all along its length. I find out later it was once a chapel. River people who worked on the Seine used to thank the river gods or whatever gods they could count on for help there.

I pay M. Teurnier the two thousand francs, counting them out until there are only two bills left in my hand. He pulls a pencil from his "blues" pocket and writes his name, address and phone number. With his thumb, he points to the boat, then with his finger points to his chest. I get the message: If I need help, call. They drive off. I hope one of them is the designated driver, but that doesn't sound very French.

An Impossible Task

I spend two days checking everything to see if the boat's still leaking. It seems OK. I hose down and clean out the interior, checking to see where the leaks were, and to a small degree, still are. Meanwhile, I'm cleaning all my furniture off in the river, trying to wash off the worst of the mud. Then, after I've dragged all the dried-out and falling-apart furniture, along with the mostly dry mattresses, sheets, and so forth back on the boat, I remount all the floating doors. I'm ready to leave. My raggedy skin has mostly peeled off, and I'm dead weary, sick and tired, with the boat, with myself.

I stop by at the Le Clercs' and ask if they'll keep an eye on my *péniche* for me. They aren't too happy about the idea, but agree to phone the farmhouse near the mill if anything goes wrong. I give them the number. They're both worried about *voleurs,* that is, robbers. I hate to tell them, but at this point I'd be glad if somebody would come along and steal the entire shebang. I've investigated, and it would cost a minimum of fifteen hundred francs to have the boat towed away and burned. That's what they do with witches and witchcraft anyway, isn't it?

I sleep two days when I'm back with the family. The stone tent seems incredibly luxurious. I carefully try recouping my tan. When I arrived, my wife said I looked like a giant fetus, or a very premature baby. I *feel* damned premature.

I decide the only thing, against all advice, is to try stopping the leak from inside the boat. What else? I ask my older boy, Matt, who's in high school, if he will help me with it on weekends. It doesn't seem to scare him. Ah, youth, good spirits and enthusiasm; we'll lick those devils and witches yet.

When we come back up to the boat from the mill, the hull has water in it, too much water for comfort, but it isn't listing. We bail one whole day. After much asking around, we find a product guaranteed to be waterproof. Happily, Matt speaks excellent French. He has lived most of his life in France. He went to French schools for the first seven years of his education. Rosemary, my wife, speaks excellent "Ma Perkins" French, as do most French teachers in American high schools, but I have virtually no skills in language. I can bumble about in French, German, Italian and Spanish, but can't speak much of any of them. The happy part is that I understand much better than I speak, not always, especially in a complex area such as the resuscitation of our boat, unhappily.

We buy fifty-liter canisters and wind up with twenty huge containers of this black, gooey, smelly stuff. We pull up all the regular flooring in the boat and pour this goop into the hold, smearing it with broad spatulas into every nook and cranny. On top of this, we jam in panels of plywood smeared with it, then work in more of this black gunk over them, again everywhere we can reach. It seems as if it should work. Foolish optimism strikes again.

We came home black as minstrels. The only thing we find that takes this goo off is turpentine. We give each other turpentine rubdowns with old towels. But around our eyes and in our cuticles and nails, including toe cuticles, we're black as coal miners. Matt's wonderful about it, going to school each Monday looking as if he's just come up from some Texas oil well drilling operation. By Friday evening, just when we're starting to look normal, we go back at it again. I can't coax the girls, or my wife, near this messy operation. I don't want to, it seems so futile. Some things are too much; this project comes in the "too much" category.

I manage to buy a small, used electric water pump. We attach an automatic float to turn it on, just in case water starts seeping in again. I have a length of plastic tubing to carry the water out the window and into the Seine, where it belongs. This allows me to sleep somewhat easier nights, but the jinxed boat continues to leak, not "sink-leak," but there's persistent, consistent dripping, a small puddle of water floating on our "impermeable" black coating each day. And we can*not* find from where it's seeping. The whole affair is maddening.

Then, one day, as we're scraping and shoveling out mud from everything, checking our pump regularly, our summer renter of the boat arrives. She's not drowned, she's fresh in a pair of toreador pants and a flowered shirt. I scramble up the bank to find out how the boat sank, what happened; is she all right. She smiles. She explains in her delightfully accented French English.

"Well, I woke late and went across the street for some croissants and a cup of coffee. I didn't need to be at the *foire* until one. When I came back, the boat was on the bottom, oop la! I didn't know what to do, and I was already late to work. So, I plucked one of the most beautiful roses from the bank and threw it onto the top of the boat. It was sort of like a Viking funeral, you see."

I don't see! It's like "you know." People keep saying "you know" at the end of just about every sentence, and most of the time I *don't* know, but they're really not interested in whether I do or not.

"But couldn't you have called to tell me what had happened? It seems the least you could do."

"I had your address in my address book, and I'd left it in the boat. I only knew you were in the Bourgogne somewhere, and no one around seemed to know your address.

"By the way, do you have any insurance? I lost quite a bit of clothing along with my thesis and my typewriter."

"No, I don't have insurance, I'd just bought the boat. You can look through the junk I've pulled out and dried off. They're piled here on the bank or in the boat. It's an awful mess, is all I can say. I didn't see any typewriter, and if I did, I doubt very much it would ever work again. Everything was totally saturated with mud."

"Oh, well, that's all right. I guess these things just happen. I'd better rush to work now."

With that, she's off, probably to some other *foire* in some other part of France. Maybe I should have told her why the boat sunk, about that damned powdered board, but I don't think it would have meant anything to her anyway.

The Diaper Caper

It's becoming clear we can never really stop the leak in the hold of the boat, at least not from inside. I'm becoming more and more desperate. Then, that week, an old friend and client for my paintings comes to Paris from California for a visit. He's shocked at what he sees. Except for our family, and those wonderful Canadians, it's the first real sympathy I feel. I tell him about my wild-ass, last-gasp solution to the leak problem. I've been lying in bed nights, trying to work my way out of this mess.

My friend, whose name is Arthur, manages and is in charge of research and development for a PCV-extruder plant in East Los Angeles. I ask if it would be possible to make a heavy-duty pool-type cover with grommets all around that I could then slip under the boat like a giant diaper. A huge smile wraps around his face under his thick wire-rim glasses when I tell him the idea. He admits it's a fascinating and possible solution, only it would be expensive. I figured on that.

"How much would it be, Arthur?"

I might as well know the worst. He looks at me, eyes twinkling, behind those milk-bottle glasses.

"How about two of the best paintings you've done this year. I'll let you choose. I don't have much time—I need to be at a conference in Geneva tomorrow. How's that for a deal?"

"You're on. I can't thank you enough, Arthur. The only thing which permits me to accept this wonderful gift is I know the paintings will be worth more than the pool cover, the boat, and most of this river before we're both dead."

We measure all around, and Arthur writes it down in a small notebook.

"I'll even send it air freight. I have a special rate through the company. It should be here within two weeks. What color do you want, blue or green?"

"Green to match the Seine."

"That water looks more black than green to me."

"OK, then black."

"No, we'll be optimistic and make it green. Maybe by the time those paintings are worth all you say they'll be, the Seine will be green again."

Arthur didn't know how predictive he was.

Two weeks later, I receive a call from a transporter for air freight. Luckily, Matt's home so he can translate for me. Trying to understand a Frenchman on the phone is quite a task, no pantomime. He says he has a package addressed to me and wants to know if I want it delivered. He claims there are customs duties to be paid as well as his transportation costs. I tell Matt what to ask, I'm already suspicious.

"How much are the customs duties, monsieur?"

Matt's face falls. The customs duty is sixteen hundred francs, about four hundred dollars. I don't have anything nearly like that. I know the package is the pool cover I've been waiting for. I ask Matt to tell the man we'll come out to look at it ourselves. Matt smiles at me.

"We'll come out to look at this package. Who, by the way,

would authorize anyone to pay customs on something like this without having seen what's in this package?"

Matt tells me the transporter is furious. He says he's already paid and can't realize the money back from customs. Matt winks at me; he's enjoying himself.

"That's your problem. You should have consulted us first." We both smile.

After some more hassle, he admits he could probably recoup the customs duty money, but we need to come sign some papers. He tells us the number of the air-freight terminal where the package is being held at Le Bourget. Also, he tells us that after tomorrow, there will be storage bills to pay as well. What a farce.

Next morning, I'm working my way through the twists and turns at Le Bourget to Freight Terminal A5. I have Matt with me. One day missed at school isn't going to matter; he's not complaining. After several false leads, we find the warehouse where they'd put the package. The warehouse is huge! The package is huge, too. The officials there want to know what a "pool cover" is. That's what Arthur had written on the customs form. Matt tries to explain. I want them to open the package. Matt is telling them what we intend doing with it. The customs officer keeps repeating, "Pool cover? *Qu'est-ce que c'est?*"

There's a woman at a desk nearby. She says clearly, *"Piscine. C'est pour une piscine."*

Matt smiles and verifies. The man talks through and around poor Matt, insists we must pay the customs duty.

I have Matt tell him it isn't worth that much. We don't have money to pay. It becomes apparent after much back and forthing that we aren't getting anywhere. He's not going to accommodate us. The freight man is in a sweat. He has the papers for me to sign so he can recuperate his money. I don't give a damn, once in a while these middlemen need to lose. I reach over and sign the papers with a large X. I turn to Matt.

"Tell him it's all his. If he wants, he can cut it up into small pieces and use it for *papier hygiénique*. He can *"pisc-ine"* it if he wants, I don't care, let's get the hell out of here."

I turn away quickly and stride out from the customs house. Matt is about to *"pisc-ine"* his pants. He's sure the cops are going to chase us. Even so, we're both torn between being scared stiff and laughing our heads off. Matt keeps looking out the back window, but there's nobody following us. I wonder what the customs man told his wife over dinner that night.

That's the end of "operation diaper." I'll never know if it would have worked. I can't imagine what they'll do with such an odd-shaped, huge pool cover, either. I don't care too much. I write and tell Arthur what's happened. He phones back, laughing. He's sympathetic, but he still wants his paintings.

A Visit to a Graveyard and a Decapitated Dragon

We go back to the boat, and there're about six inches of water in the bottom of the hull, the automatic pump didn't turn on. We prime it till it's working again and bail like crazy. Two hours later, the hull is more or less dry. *I'm* going more or less berserk! I've reached the point of having the boat destroyed after all.

The next day I receive a phone call. It's from M. Teurnier. He says he has something to show me. He's downriver from me and he'll pick me up and take me to his boatyard. He also says he'll drive me back in the afternoon. This is all tough to get across on the phone, especially without the pantomime. Under duress, my French must be improving. I'm hoping I understood him correctly, there are so many different ways I could be wrong. I'm also wishing I had Matt with me. It's the story of my life apparently— my boat life, anyway—half the time not understanding what's going on, and what I do understand isn't going well at all.

I'm doing some adjusting on my little pump and bailing more water out when M. Teurnier arrives promptly as he said he would. He pulls up to the bank where I've been trying to glue my furniture back together.

He goes down the bank past me and looks around the inside of the boat. He comes out shaking his head and motions me to climb into his rattletrap of a car. His head just about clears the dash so he can see out the windshield. To make it possible, he has three ragged pillows to boost himself up on, giving him a few centimeters of height, and half a chance.

The seats in the back of the car have been ripped out, and the space is filled with grease-smeared tools and pieces of cut metal. He drives the way a madman should.

After half an hour of twisting, turning driving, we stop in the middle of nowhere. His house turns out to be a houseboat pulled up onto a section of land, a sort of small island between branches of the meandering Seine. He pantomimes with his arms how the river rises with floods.

It turns out, he moved his boat up onto the land when the flood was high, then, as the water went down, he built concrete foundations under his boat. He laughs and slaps his knee as he tells this. It certainly makes for a peculiar-looking house.

We go inside and I meet his wife, who speaks a little English. She tells me their daughter is studying English at school and will be home soon. It turns out the daughter will translate. M. Teurnier pulls me by the arm down to one of the riverbanks. I can see this is the equivalent of a boat cemetery. There are half-sunken rusty boats everywhere, from rowboats to enormous barges. They're all rusting into nothingness. Men are cutting and arc-welding on all sides. The smell of burnt metal dominates everything, even the foul smell of the river.

M. Teurnier is dragging me over to an abortion of a filthy barge. To me it looks something like a giant sea dragon with its head cut off. It's rusted everywhere, and where there isn't rust, there are streaks and puddles of oil smeared haphazardly.

Now I know this kind of thing might be heaven to a real boat person, but it looks hellish to me. Before I acquired my sinking violet of a wooden boat, my marine experience had been limited to some rowing of rowboats in parks, a few fishing trips on hired fishing boats off the Jersey shore, two half-day excursions in Arthur's sailboat out of the marina in Los Angeles, and playing with boats in my bathtub as a child. What I'm seeing in front of me is an unmitigated horror. I find myself flinching, I want to escape.

But, M. Teurnier leads me across a watery canyon between the bank and this filthy wreck. He's jabbering away and gesticulating all the time. Lord, what am I getting myself into now?

I'm looking back to the comforts of M. Teurnier's goofy boathouse up on stilts, on dry land, searching for some remnants of sanity. It's then I see what seems to me like a scene from an Ingmar Bergman film. A small girl in a pinafore is running, jumping and skipping over this desolate landscape littered with rusting, sharp shards of boats and parts of boats. She's shouting as she comes.

"Papa!"

A French Angel Named Corinne

M. Teurnier's face lights up and he winks at me. He moves over to the narrow plank bridge onto this derelict boat, but there's no need. She lightly dances across it the way her father did. She runs into his arms, seemingly unaware of the contrast between her beautiful ruffled dress, covered by her school *tablier,* a sort of apron, compared to her dad's mud-, sweat- and oil-covered "blues." He gives her a swing in the air. I assume she is to be our translator for whatever there is to translate. I'm right.

She pushes her face up to me for the typical Breton three kisses. I manage it, but I'm almost pulled off my footing on this slippery deck covered with various unplanned, unannounced booby traps. I almost fall into her. She appears to be about eleven years old and is absolutely bursting with enthusiasm. She looks me right straight in the eyes, hers blue as old M. Teurnier's must have been fifty years ago. M. Teurnier speaks to her quickly, and she turns to me.

"Ah, you are the American who has a boat *mon père* lifted out of the water."

Her accent is quite good. She speaks clearly and with verve.

"Yes, that's right, little one. What is your name?"

"I am called Corinne. Mama says I should tell you what Papa is trying to tell you."

So, from then on, M. Teurnier speaks and she, haltingly but carefully, translates. She's really rather amazing.

It seems this old shell of a hull I'm standing on had once been an oil barge, hauling oil from Le Havre to different ports along the canals that traverse all of France. The boat was built sixty years ago and had been in service every day since, until recently. This part is easy. Then she points out, at M. Teurnier's instruction, that the plates of steel forming the boat are riveted, not welded. He points to rivets all over the hull. This, apparently, is good. We look down an open hatch into a deep pitch-black interior. I knew it was a hell. We move to the other end of the boat. It really has had the head cut off, but the beheaded dragon isn't bleeding. In fact, it's still shining metal where the surgery was performed. Saint George would be proud.

This part is hard for Corinne to translate. Her father has his arms going like a windmill, trying to explain. It's so complicated, I can just barely hang on.

It seems that boats like this, standard barges, thirty-nine meters long, are no longer practical on the rivers and canals. They cannot carry enough cargo, and it takes three people to run them safely, especially going through the many locks.

This part I understand reasonably well. Then, with the windmilling of M. Teurnier and Corinne's stumbling, halting search for words, I gather that they cut off the part of this boat with the motor and cabin, along with two of the oil-storage sections. The idea was to convert it into a "pusher." It will push four empty barges, without motors, along the river. Then, three people running it can make four times as much money as before. They cannot carry oil, only grain, sand, gravel or coal, but that's enough.

M. Teurnier points across his no-man's-land to what I assume is the onetime head of this monster boat. Men are climbing over it, cutting, welding, pounding. I figure this will be the "pusher."

Then M. Teurnier starts marching along the length of this beheaded boat beneath us. It's still enormous, even with the amputation. He shows me that it's about seventy feet long. At intervals there are bulging, complex sorts of metal bubbles. Corinne explains they are the pumps that pumped the oil into and out of the barge when it functioned, before it was turned into a metal corpse. M. Teurnier makes swinging, chopping motions to show how he would cut these off. It looks impossible, but little Corinne verifies.

Now he takes me to the other end of the boat. There's a raised hatch cover and a steep boat-type ladder staircase going down into the dark. He whips out a flashlight he had strapped to his waist and motions me to follow. Down there, it's almost sane. A bed is fitted against one wall, a sink, some varnished mahogany cabinets, and a built-in bench with storage under it, along another wall. All the fittings are beautiful shined brass. Corinne explains this was the crew cabin. We go upstairs onto the deck mayhem again.

Now, M. Teurnier goes down into that dark hole. He motions for me to follow. It's a metal ladder with thin, round iron rungs, standing almost vertically against the hatch opening. M. Teurnier obviously tells Corinne to stay on deck or she'll soil her frock. She wants to come down, but he repeats *"non."* That frock is still freshly clean, despite all. When we are belowdecks, he signals with his flashlight for me to stand with him on two boards balanced across a pair of boxes about six feet apart. The entire bottom of the boat is thick with oil, oil the consistency of mud. He starts waving his flashlight around at the black walls. The space seems small for the size of the boat upstairs. I'm on the edge of panic that I'm going to fall off these wiggling boards into the morass around us. I can't guess how deep this glistening pool of oil might be.

M. Teurnier realizes I'm not understanding all his jabbering. Corinne is still above us, her beautiful face peering into the murky darkness. It must be how an angel would appear if one were looking up from the depths of hell. M. Teurnier gives a long spiel directed up at his daughter. She translates for me by putting her small hands around her mouth like a megaphone. Sounds rattle around and reverberate against the walls in the hull of the boat.

It seems the boat originally had six individual compartments for the oil. There are four left; we're in one of them. There are two on a side, two in a row. I'm actually only looking at less than a quarter of the space involved.

He explains through Corinne that the back walls of the last compartments have a wall as strong against water as the hull itself. After all, they held oil. They too are riveted. There's a bit of confusion then, but Corinne works it out.

M. Teurnier wants me to know that because this hull has always had its metal soaked in oil, it has never rusted. It's like a new hull. This sounds far-fetched, but I don't care, none of this means anything to me. It's his problem; why is he telling me about it? He also makes a big point that the boat was usually full or empty, so the waterline, the part where there is the most damage to a hull, would not be a factor in my case. A factor in what?! I'm beginning to smell the rat. This is not just a tour of an old, chopped-up, oil-filled half-assed barge being provided for my enlightenment and entertainment. This is a sales pitch. We're doing business.

Monkey Business

To my relief, we climb up out of the hull. M. Teurnier is like a monkey—he goes up and over the edge onto the deck as if he's in a circus or a zoo. I gingerly mount the slippery, round-runged metal ladder to the deck and am forced to crawl on my hands and knees to push myself upright, so now I have filthy hands and jeans. Corinne is ladylike enough to suppress a giggle.

Well, now that I've had the tour, we knuckle down to the real business. M. Teurnier is convinced this derelict of a boat is the answer to my problem. It sounds to me like taking on a demanding, ugly mistress when one already has a demanding, beautiful, suspicious, although somewhat ailing wife.

Little Corinne goes on with the translating. His idea is that first we cut off all these pump bumps on deck. Then we cut out the entire center wall dividing the left from the right half of the interior hull all the way from crew cabin to the amputated back of the boat. He holds up a cautioning finger and warns that we must leave enough for structural support. This is all becoming embarrassingly hilarious. How am I ever going to get out of this insanity?

After that, he claims we'll cut doorways in the horizontal wall, making the whole thing into one gigantic hull. He wants me to come down into the hull again to see how this scenario would work.

I'm listening. It's all fascinating, but this entire scheme seems so wild, so expensive, so beyond anything I could ever manage, I'm totally turned off. I'm wondering how I can escape from this lunatic. I turn to little Corinne.

"Tell your daddy that his ideas sound marvelous, but I don't have any cutting or welding equipment or any tools to work with metal. Even if I did have these tools, I've no idea how to use them. Also, it sounds too expensive. I don't have much money."

She smiles, then makes a cute funny face at me. She begins to translate. But the big smile that comes across M. Teurnier's face doesn't look like that of a man who's just had a grand scheme, a business deal, shot down. He stares smiling into my eyes. He motions little Corinne and me to follow him.

We go back across that treacherous plank. I'm trying not to look down. Then we walk across the minefield of cut and rusting metal to his house on blocks in the middle of it all. He invites me inside. His wife is cooking. She turns as we come in, smiles and says "Hello" in English.

M. Teurnier is casting his eyes about looking for something, then he speaks to Corinne. She takes out her leather school bag, pulls from it a thin notebook with pale blue lines up and down, back and forth. Then she gives him a ballpoint pen, but he reaches into his breast pocket and pulls out a greasy grease pencil, about half an inch thick and flat. He reaches into another pocket, extracts a fisherman's folding knife and sharpens the pencil, pulling the blade toward his chest. He's talking all the time, more or less muttering to himself. Corinne doesn't bother to translate. She shrugs.

Mme. Teurnier motions me to sit at the oilcloth-covered table in the center of the room. Corinne is leaning against the other side of it, then she sits down. M. Teurnier is sitting beside me. He's starting to make a list. After each item on the list, he sucks the tip of his pencil, then writes a number. Corinne comes around and starts translating from the list. I can almost hear the enthusiastic timbre of M. Teurnier's voice in her clear thin one.

"See. I'll sell you that entire barge at the price of scrap metal. That's what I'd need to do anyway. It's dead now, the name of the barge, *Ste.-Margarite*, went to the pusher."

He looks into my eyes to see if I'm understanding. I'm not really. He points at the numbers beside the first item on the list. I read. He's written 270,000 francs. That's what it looks like to me with the seven crossed French style. That's about what I thought would be involved. Then, as I'm about to give up totally, he puts in a comma after the *second* zero from the end. This is now 2,700 francs, at that time less than eight hundred dollars. That's ridiculously low. I take the pencil from his hand, and beside his number write 2,700 NF, even crossing the seven. The French at that time (still) tended to quote big numbers in old francs. He looks at me and smiles. I smile. This is beginning to look vaguely possible, very vaguely.

Then again he talks to his cute little girl. It's obvious she's becoming bored with the whole business. But still I hear his vital voice through her. She's going down the list, changing all the numbers into new francs. She's impressive all right.

"To cut the pumps off the deck, three hundred. To cut out the walls of the compartments, six hundred. To move the barge down to where your sinking wooden boat is, now, in Port Marly, five hundred."

M. Teurnier pauses, looks at the ceiling, sucks his pencil again. I wait. He writes the number down. Corinne translates.

"To put the two boats together, your boat on top of this one, one thousand new francs."

I'm bewildered. He licks the point of his pencil and starts adding the numbers. He comes up with 5,100 new francs. He looks up at me, then knocks off the hundred francs.

He talks quickly to Corinne, who's now sitting her doll in a tiny high chair at the table. From there she tells me what he's saying. She's getting more fluent with each exchange. I'm really surprised that she still plays with dolls. French children seem to play longer than American children. I will say again, she'll make a great translator someday, dolls and all.

"My father says the boat, with all the work, will only cost you five thousand new francs. If you need to have your old boat pulled away and destroyed, it would cost you twenty-five hundred francs. This way you can have a big two-story boat with much space for just twice that price.

"Father also says, when the boats are together, he will send his brother out to cut windows in the barge, around both sides, for only five hundred francs more. He'll also cut away the inside walls."

She looks at me and smiles.

"But, he says first you must remove all the oil in the bottom of the boat so the work can take place. He knows a man who will bring barrels and has a way to lift them away. This man uses the oil to make roads. This will cost you nothing."

This entire business is totally unreal. None of it is making sense to me, but at the same time, I'm excited. He holds up his hand again. He's hurrying. I can see his wife has the midday meal ready and is becoming impatient. He machine-gun-talks the rest of the deal. Corinne tries to keep up, but it's almost impossible.

"The oil must be out in three weeks, or a month at most. I have workers, welders, metalworkers, who will be needing work by then. Also, you must move the boat from the atelier here to Port Marly."

I look up at Corinne and smile. I smile at Mme. Teurnier. She indicates the table with her hands.

"Please eat with us, monsieur."

Jack and the Beanstalk

M. Teurnier backs up the invitation with broad motions of his arms. He pulls another chair over to the table. It's the first time I've been invited to share a French meal. I don't know what's the right thing to do. Corinne breaks the deadlock.

"You have no automobile; you cannot go home until Papa drives you, so you must dine with us."

Over a magnificent but simple meal, we review the details again. I keep staring at the numbers, wondering from whom I can borrow the money, how I'll ever pay it back.

When we finish, I ask if I can use their phone. I call Rosemary at school, something I virtually never do. She comes dashing in from her kindergarten expecting the worst. Maybe this is the worst. I've lost all track.

"Rosemary, I'm involved in the most complicated, interesting, extravagant arrangement to save our boat and make it more than twice its size and with a metal hull. I've just had lunch with M. Teurnier and his family, and I'm using their phone."

She's quiet on the other end, giving off vibes of impatience. One can't leave kindergartners for more than a few minutes. I start to explain the price structure as I understand it. She interrupts.

"Dear, can you please wait till I come home? I need to go back in my class right now. You do what you think is right. I'll go along with anything to stop you from tossing and turning the whole night through. Goodbye."

I look into the hole of the phone. I pause a moment to think. I make up my mind, walk over to M. Teurnier with my hand out. We shake. He puts his other hand on top of mine and winks at me. What does that wink have to do with it? He looks like a combination of Popeye and a worn-out midget version of Yves Montand. He speaks through the little girl. He faces me and she says the words. She's preparing to go back to school, has her pack on her back.

"We are *les frères Teurnier.* My father started this business."

He holds up his hand with four fingers extended.

"These are my brothers."

He names them. He untucks his thumb and holds it out in the French sign for victory, success.

"This is me, Jacques Teurnier. You will not be sorry to work with us."

When I come home to the apartment after stopping to bail and pump the boat, I sit down at dinner and explain everything to the family as best I can with my limited understanding.

Again, despite my careful description of the enormity of this task, the ugliness of the barge, there's enthusiasm. Matt says he and Tom, his best friend, will help with cleaning out the bottom of the barge. I try to make clear the horrendous dimensions of the job, but I take him up on it. I know I could never do it myself.

Just before he left me off at my boat, M. Teurnier told me that soon as he drove back to his boatyard, he'd have some of his men cut the pumps off the decks so we'd have light down in the hold. He also told me he'd manage to gather ten large oil drums to be put on the quay beside the boat. Those will be for dumping the oil into, and he promises to have them hauled away each week. Ten drums of oil a week? What have I gotten us into?! This could take up the rest of my life. All this would be ready by the weekend.

That Saturday, we all—the whole family plus Tom—go out to the boatyard. This involves much searching through unfamiliar territory over dirt roads, but we manage. I find the barge. We make the perilous trip through the boatyard and look at it. Rosemary gives me one of her "I-don't-believe-this!" looks. That'll teach her to give me free rein on barmy projects.

We each walk the gangplank onto the barge and peer down into the hold. M. Teurnier, true to his word, has had the pumps cut off, so the deck is clear except for four traplike holes rimmed with jagged steel. But now we can see down into each of the sections. He has also arranged for the oil drums.

We can see there must be close to a foot of thick, black, viscous oil over the entire floor of the hold, in each section. I feel like Jack of *Jack and the Beanstalk,* showing the beans I've received for the family cow.

Matt, Tom and I have had the good sense to dress in bathing suits and old-time bathing caps. We have a few shovels, some trowels, and, at Rosemary's insistence, two dustpans. Those dustpans prove invaluable. We also have three buckets to put the black goop into and carry it up the ladder.

After much experimentation, by the end of which we look like miners coming up from the pits of Newcastle, we work out a rotating chain, one scooping the goop into the bucket, then passing it along to another in mid-ladder. After that, it's passed up to Kate, our oldest, who's figured a way to slide the bucket across the deck, then along the gangplank to the edge, where Rosemary helps her dump it into an oil drum. It's sloppy, splashy work.

That first day, we fill four oil drums, not counting what's smeared all over our bodies. I've brought three bottles of white spirits, and we clean the worst of it off, but it stings. We rub each other hard with old towels. Then we spread newspapers over the inside of our car and drive home quite dispiritedly (except for our stinging skin).

So Much for Science

The next weekend we're better prepared. That first time, we'd packed lunches, but we couldn't eat them because anything we touched became covered with oil. We also have everybody in bathing suits and shower caps this time, and pack more old towels. We fill six drums before lunch. We're quite proud of ourselves, It's like a war. Rosemary's made sandwiches cut into bite sizes and wrapped in pieces of paper towel. Lunch is a matter of carefully working the mini-sandwiches out, so the paper towel keeps the taste of oil off them. We have an individual bottle of water for each of us. The necks of the bottles become black, smeared by our oil-covered lips.

We work until dark, filling ten barrels altogether. We can begin to see we're making progress, but slowly. We have one section empty down to the hull and another started. The job isn't impossible, it's only intolerable.

When we reach home, I can feel my back wanting to go out. I've alternated, as have the others, between standing barefoot (the only way) on the bottom of the hull, scooping oil into buckets, or standing halfway up the ladder in oil-begrimed boots, passing the heavy buckets up. This might be all right for a seventeen- or eighteen-year-old boy, but this boy is over forty. Sometimes I can fool myself, but I can't fool my back.

I'm in bed all that week, and when we go out the next weekend, I'm wearing my old back brace. It's going to be smeared with oil, too. Poor Rosemary soaks our swimsuits, shower caps and socks in white spirits, then soaks them in soapy water after each session. The boys are beginning to lose enthusiasm, naturally, and we try bucking each other up with songs of labor. "Yo Ho Heave Ho" or "Tote That Barge, Lift That Bale" seem to be the favorites. It helps.

Worst of all, both Matt and Tom begin to break out in gigantic boils all over their backs. It's almost impossible, even in a hot shower with cleansing powder—we can't scrub the oil out of our skin. Each Monday, the boys arrive at school looking like terminal cases with a terrible disease, dark rings around their eyes, hair sticky and discolored, boils flaring away. And then, as with the goo Matt and I spread all over the hull of the wooden boat, just when we start looking almost human, it's back to the barge.

But believe it or not, we do pull out all that oil in four weekends. M. Teurnier is beginning to be impatient. I don't think he figured on a family act. We're all sore, filthy, but impressed with ourselves. Next week, M. Teurnier will push or pull our metal boat along the fifty twisting kilometers, through the locks, between where it is now and Port Marly, where the sinking wooden boat awaits. They'll be starting at six in the morning Wednesday to avoid some of the crowds at the locks.

I really don't yet believe, or understand, how they can hoist my wooden boat up onto the metal hull. I don't want to think about it even. But I have. I just haven't enough French to ask, and I'm worried.

We have two longtime friends in Paris who are scientists. One, of Russian background, named Serge, might well be the most optimistic person I know. My experience with Russians, in general, is that they are pessimistic, but Serge is the raving exception. He, of all things, is in charge of collecting cosmic dust for the French. He has ships floating all over the world gathering this dust. Would you believe it?

But he's a world-respected scientist. I give him all the information I have, center of gravity, buoyancy, weights, heights, everything I can gather I think might be appropriate. I explain the actual physical project, that is, putting my sinking wooden boat onto the partial hull of an old oil barge.

Serge tilts his head quizzically, does a few quick calculations and gives his somewhat studied opinion.

"It will not float. The entire combination will tip over, and your boat will be in the water upside down. There is, unfortunately, no other possibility."

Serge has been in France long enough, so there is nothing halfway about him—it's all or nothing. I'm about to give in, but I go to my other scientist.

This one is American. He was once in charge of the particle accelerator at Berkeley. He's now working for a large oil company with offices in the fancy business section of La Défense. He's a research scientist, a physicist.

I go visit him at his office. He's most cordial, though generally a somewhat morose man, definitely a pessimist. I present my data to him. I don't mention my other scientific opinion.

His name is Roger. Roger fills two pages of lined yellow paper with notations meaning nothing to me. I don't recognize a single word in either French or English. He looks me in the eye with his sad eyes. I should say here, he has a strong resemblance to Dr. Oppenheimer. He gives me what passes for a smile from a pessimist, a sort of double twist of the lips, a lifted eyebrow over lowered eyes, and delivers his report.

"You don't have a worry in the world. There's absolutely no way the relatively light weight of the small boat you intend to place on the deck of the metal boat could possibly effect the stability of that barge. Go right to it and good luck."

So there I am. We're to start the marriage of the two boats in a few days. I drive out to M. Teurnier's place with the rest of the money I owe him. I'm deeply in hock to three generous friends, none of them scientists, none of them artists, but all of them lovers of the arts, and here I am counting out 5,500 francs in five-hundred-franc bills. I must be out of my mind.

I explain to M. Teurnier, with Corinne's help, my scientific discoveries. He laughs. He's just finishing his lunch and has a huge piece of bread in his mouth. He almost chokes, then swallows. He waves his arms at me, signaling little Corinne to stay on and finish her dessert while he leads the crazy American outside to the boatyard.

We go hopping and hobbling alone to another section of the yard, where I haven't been. He points. I see a barge, and on the barge is a gigantic yellow crane. On one end of the crane is a barge being lifted practically out of the water, over the *side* of the first barge! I can't believe it. We look at each other. He laughs and I start laughing, too. So much for science. He puts his hand on my shoulder; it's quite a reach for him. I'm convinced. I don't want to interfere with his meal anymore. I feel somewhat foolish. We make our definite plans for the boat marriage.

———

The Marriage

At last comes the day of the great event. It's a Saturday and a crowd of our friends are there to watch what seems to be this impending catastrophe. That is everyone except poor Matt. Two evenings before, bailing with me, he sprained or broke his ankle. We had dashed off to the emergency room at the American Hospital, and sure enough, it was a hairline fracture. This boat is definitely jinxed. But there's no stopping now.

I know that when my friends see the cockeyed enormity of this whole thing, they're shocked. I'm shocked myself. There, back in the boat cemetery, it almost made sense. Here, it's a nightmare in black and white with no subtitles.

Matt has just arrived on crutches and has stretched out on the bank, when I see a flat-topped boat floating downriver. On it stands the entire Teurnier mob, feet apart, hands on hips, except for the one at the wheel. Behind them, being towed, is my barge. I go down by the water's edge to greet them. They have the air of grown men at a picnic. Teurnier shakes hands with me, and the others shake with me in turn. He's started issuing commands left and right. Matt slides down the hill, even with his cast and crutches. He acts as translator.

"See, Dad, first they're going to anchor the barge crossways on the river, blocking traffic; they've gotten permission from *le chef de navigation* for this. Then, they're going to pump river water through the holes on the deck into the metal barge until it sinks."

So, I'm to have another sunken boat, just what I need. Matt turns again and checks with M. Teurnier as if to verify this absurd action.

"He says don't worry, the crew cabin is watertight and won't sink. So, one end of the boat, the front end, will still be sticking up. He wants *you* out there."

They've already, with great efficiency, positioned the metal barge cross river and started pumping water into it. They then manipulate my small, pitiful wooden boat up to it, using their boat as a tug, cross river, just upriver, from the metal barge. They're also using the motor of their boat to keep the current from pulling the two boats downriver to Le Havre. The whole affair is something like a monstrous rodeo of barges. Matt's shouting translations to me.

"Then Dad, you see, they're sinking the metal barge to the bottom. After that, they'll pull our wooden boat up on top of the metal barge. Dad, are you sure you want to try this? It sounds so goofy and dangerous."

"I'm in for it, Matt, ludicrous as it might seem. There's no backing out now."

I climb up onto the roof of my wooden boat and Teurnier throws me a rope that has been attached to a bollard on my now almost completely sunken metal barge. I can feel my heart sinking as it sinks to the bottom. They certainly go down faster than they come up. I feel as if I have a whale on the end of a light fishing line. M. Teurnier's hollering to Matt. Matt turns to me.

"The idea is they're going to pull you in this boat over the metal barge, and you'll be the one to sight along the two boats to see if they're lined up properly. At least, I'm almost sure that's what he's saying. You be careful, Dad!"

Matt turns out to be right. With much pushing and pulling, and short bursts of the motor on the boat they used for pulling and pushing the metal boat down here, we do line up our wooden boat on top of the barge, at least as far as I can see through the dimness of the filthy, black water. It's a hot day for fall, and I'm wearing only shorts. I'm dripping sweat. I'm not actually doing anything, so it must be nervousness.

Now I'm standing on the stern of the metal barge, up on the hatch over the crew cabin, peering down the length of our wooden boat, checking each side to see if it's lined up on the sinking barge underneath.

They work the wooden boat higher and higher up the ramp of the slanted, sunken deck of the barge until the bow end is within two meters of the opening to the crew cabin. Now I'm to give the signal when it looks to me as if we're in line. I'm an artist, so I should be able to estimate if two objects are parallel and in line, but this is the ultimate test.

Finally, in a desperation of indecision, I give the signal. The pumps start, pulling water out of the metal hull. Wooden covers have been tied over the openings where the oil pumps once were. These old oil pumps are probably already starting to fester with rust in that Père Lachaise–like cemetery for boats at M. Teurnier's.

As the barge rises slowly, the upper boat settles onto the deck of the metal hull, and the wooden covers are removed one by one. The idea apparently is that the boat, our wooden boat, will now block water from seeping in while the pumps are pushing it out. It's all so ingenious. I'm no use at all. I should be up on the bank with the audience, applauding or cheering, laughing or crying.

I've been worried that we haven't done anything actually to attach the wooden boat to the metal boat. I yell over at Matt to have him ask M. Teurnier about it. Teurnier starts explaining to me, then throws up his arms and turns to Matt. He rattles on for about five minutes, making arm motions and finger signals as if he's a giant tomcat trying to catch a mouse hanging from a string over his head. When it ends, Matt begins.

"This is wild, Dad. The idea is basically that the hatch covers were cut so they have sharp edges. When the wooden boat is finally lowered down onto them, these edges will cut into the oak bottom of the upper boat. He's convinced this will hold the boat in place. He insists our wooden boat isn't going anywhere."

Matt is making the same kind of clawlike upward motions with his hands Teurnier was making. It seems sort of precarious to me, but it's too late now, and what else could we do anyway?

———

I'm at the highest part of the whole convoluted, bizarre complex, up on the roof of the covered hatch to the crew cabin of the lower boat, holding on to the high edge of the wooden boat's roof. I look along the entire length before me and the view is somehow sexy, a lovely white lady lover of a wooden boat, hovering over, then lowering herself gently onto this rising giant of a black bull barge in the swirling water. Powerful, forceful jets of water surge from her supine lover, spewing up and splashing down into the river.

Just then, it starts to happen. I should have kept my dirty old man's mind on the job, holding down that boat. I don't, to this day, know what actually transpired. The hull is about halfway emptied, when suddenly there's a sort of lurch, then slowly, both boats begin to tip toward the downriver side! My first thought is it's from the pressure of river water against the hull. Or, maybe my normally optimistic Russian friend was right after all.

The boats, relentlessly, persistently, continuously tip. I move slowly. I'm still, ridiculously, trying to hold my original wooden boat from sliding off into the water, which it seems to be doing, despite the supposed effect of those jagged gripping hatches.

Everybody's running around this way and that, cursing in Breton, French and general international obscenity. I don't know what they're doing, or why. M. Teurnier actually goes into the river with all his clothes on and is wrestling with something underwater. I hope he doesn't lose his skin—I'm beginning to feel I'm losing my shirt.

He comes bounding out and runs past me up the tipping metal hull on the upriver up-boat side. I'm still frantically holding on to the edge of the roof, stupidly trying to convince myself I can keep the boat from tipping off and into the water sideways. But even more, I'm holding on for dear life. As he goes by, M. Teurnier mumbles just two words, two words even I can understand, *"C'est malheureux."* In direct translation, "It's unhappy." It seems a masterpiece of understatement.

They're still pumping water out of the lower barge like madmen. I'm convinced the answer is to pump water back into the barge and start over again, or just leave the entire mess down there. I'm spinning, considering opening a restaurant, an underwater Philadelphia-hoagie restaurant specializing in "submarine" sandwiches à la Seine. What else?

Gone with the Wind

We eventually tip over to a thirty-six-degree angle from the level of the water on the high side. I measure it, later, from the watermark on the cut end of the boat.

Realizing how foolish I must look trying to hold my big wooden boat in place at an angle, I let go an instant to search for the best place where I can jump when this leaning tower of a boat gives in to gravity. That upper boat actually starts to *lift*, to tip slowly, when I let go! I grab hold with both hands and press down desperately. The captain will go down with his ship, or is that ships.

Then, for reasons I still don't understand, the tipping slows, then stops. Gently the barge rights itself. In no time at all, it's level. My leaking old wooden boat squats properly on top, more or less dry, properly placed and aligned.

I drop to my haunches on the hatch cover because my knees are so weak I can't stand. I hear the cheers of our gallery, but I'm crying and too completely pooped physically and mentally to take a bow. I'm in the stern. I'm invisible to them.

M. Teurnier comes around with a big wrench knocking along the bottom of the upper boat for some reason, maybe it's like kicking tires on an automobile. When he sees me, he breaks into a huge smile and reaches over; we shake hands. Then he winds it up with one of those masculine French hugs that can break ribs. He's

43

soaking wet, so now I am, too, combination of river and sweat. We're both laughing.

He passes me and continues around with his "tire thumping." I manage to stand alone on my wobbling legs and work my way to the other end, the shore end, of the boat. There's an apron about two feet wide on each side of the upper boat where the metal barge is wider. It makes a passable yet treacherous walkway. I hold on to anything I can find to inch myself along.

When I come to the bow of the boat, the end facing land, there's another rousing cheer. I look up and wave a hand, feeling like Jacques Cousteau. Maybe the crowd thought I was actually holding the wooden boat in place up there with my bare hands. I'll take any kudos I can get, deserved or not. Sternly, I decide not to bow in the bow. It wouldn't be seemly.

Our next maneuver is to clear out a space for our new enlarged "bastard" boat. Our old one, the wooden sinker, was only eighteen meters long. We now need to fit twenty-three meters of metal barge into the old space. There appears to be enough room between my barge and the neighboring houseboats, but that isn't exactly the dilemma.

The first difficulty is physical. It seems there's a sandbar there, which will keep my barge, much deeper in the water now than before, from squeezing into the old place. This sandbar has built up over the years. When it was only my light wooden boat, this didn't matter, but with my new, heavy, metal monster, five times as bulky, it's a serious affair. When we try easing the barge into place, it just won't fit.

The second horn of the dilemma is political, psychological, psychic, etc., but we'll come to that. I'm still shaky and covered with sweat, dirt and water. The pumps inside the metal hull are running hard, pulling out the last dregs. Two of M. Teurnier's brothers are down there, more or less vacuuming up the last of the water.

M. Teurnier explains the problem to Matt. A good part of our audience has disappeared. The show is over. That's what they think; the best (worst) is yet to come. Matt translates, explains about the sandbar. M. Teurnier wants to pull our barge out to the center of the river and bring their boat into the space. Then they'll turn on the motors full blast and blow out the sandbar. He's convinced it will work. I'm not, but what do I know, this is all in the area of hands-on nautical engineering.

So, that's what we try to do. The barge is pulled out into the center of the river and anchored somehow. Where did they find the anchor? I don't know. Then, they wedge their flat-topped boat into the space. This boat could serve as a landing field for small helicopters. They turn the double motors on full blast. Water, sand and sound fill the air.

Now comes the political, psychological, psychical part. Madame Le Clerc, our downriver neighbor, is standing perilously at the stern of her boat, shouting. But no one can hear with all the racket. She's shaking her finger at M. Teurnier and at me. I pretend not to see. What can I do? M. Teurnier bends backward at the waist with his hands on his hips and laughs at her. Oh, boy!

Next, the owner of the boat on the other side, our upriver neighbor, with the lovely pirate boat, is out on her poop deck shouting even louder. If one didn't see us between them, one would think they were having a terrible argument, shouting dementedly at each other. Too bad that isn't the case. We are caught directly in the crossfire, and we are *not* innocent bystanders.

There ensues about fifteen minutes of roaring motors, rushing water, flying sand, a wild churning up of the river. It's making a colossal stink because the propellers of the boat are releasing years of buried methane gas. It smells ten times worse than the sewers in Paris. Finally, they turn the motors off. M. Teurnier has a gaffing hook and is testing for depth. Unfortunately, now we can hear the ladies shouting. I'm glad I can't understand. I'm as deaf to what they're saying as I was with the motors roaring. Matt shakes his head and doesn't want to translate.

"Honest, Dad. I can hardly understand what they're saying and what I do understand, I don't want to try translating. You don't need to hear all this anyway. Just play dumb."

"Come on, Matt. I already am dumb, but I'll need to deal with it sooner or later."

"OK, as far as I can tell, they're both objecting to the fact that your new boat is going to take up more space than the old one. It seems the river law is that there's supposed to be five meters between each boat. Teurnier insists that when your boat is in place, there will be at least five meters on each side. I think he's right; they're only being hysterical, fighting for and defending territory."

"So what else are they saying?"

"Madame Le Clerc objects to having our old wreck of a boat beside her beautiful mansion of a boat. She's going to call *Le Navigation*. She claims Monsieur LeCerb, the boss man there, is a friend of hers."

"That sounds bad. What do they want me to do, just sink my barge again?"

"It all sounds bad, Dad. I can't exactly translate what Luce, the other lady, the one on the pirate boat, is yelling because she keeps slipping into Breton. She's the one who really seems to get M. Teurnier's goat. She's apparently bawling him out in full voice, exercising her waterfront knowledge and expertise in Breton obscenity. And all this hollering brings out the Breton in M. Teurnier. He yells back at her, sometimes in French, sometimes in Breton. The last thing he told her was if she didn't shut up and go inside, he was going to come up on that boat and give her a spanking."

"This is better than a movie. Too bad we're in it, even as extras. By the way, what happened to our audience?"

While all this is happening, the other *frères Teurnier* have been shoving our boat back into the space they've cut out. They concentrate and work, don't say a thing. They've wedged our barge close to the bank, but it's still too long and too deep in the water to fit properly. They use their boat as a tug to push it in sideways. They manage to work the front end, the downriver end, in, where the water's deeper and there's no sandbar, but the back sticks out about a meter and a half more than it should. Teurnier's pulled out a tape measure and is measuring the distances between the boats. He shouts out the measurements to each woman; there is almost six meters on each side. They screech back at him now, words even I can tell would never be approved by l'Académie française.

As it begins to grow dark, we decide to leave the boat as is, with its upriver end, the cut-off stern, sticking out. I ask Matt to translate for me. I'm desperate. They're about to leave, and I need to move the back of the barge against the *berge*. Matt listens carefully, then turns to me as they're making ready to pull out. The crew has piled a stack of equipment on the back deck of our barge. Matt looks at me through the gathering dusk.

"He says there's a dredger upriver who can come here and dredge out the rest of the sandbar. It'll probably cost another four hundred francs or so. He'll check for us.

"Also, he's left cutting tools and an arc-welding set here. Tomorrow, someone, probably one of his brothers, will come at eight in the morning to start cutting out the windows. You should be here to tell him where you want them and give him a hand. He says they shouldn't be cut closer than forty centimeters from the water level and there should be a minimum of three structural struts left in place along the sides between each window. At least that's what I think he said."

M. Teurnier and the rest of his finger-brothers are on their barge and about ready to head home. M. Teurnier stands at the stern lighting his pipe. He smiles at us between puffs. He seems happy with what he's done. My God!

He yells one last time. Matt stands on his cast, pushing himself up with his crutches. He cups his hand to his ear, picking up what Teurnier's saying over the noise of his boat's motor. Matt turns to me as they disappear.

"He says not to bother about what Mme. Le Clerc will say to the *Navigation* or M. LeCerb at the Ponts et Chaussées. Teurnier's going to stop by and see him on the way through the lock. He's convinced that will do it. You're perfectly legal."

So, there I am, with two half-assed boats joined in a naval wedlock, sort of a shotgun wedding at that. The sun is just about gone. I wander through the upper boat. It's encouraging to see it drying, but it's filthy. I wonder how I'm ever going to work my way down into the lower boat. All the hatches where the pumps have been cut off are now covered by the bottom of my wooden boat, so it's completely sealed. Also, how am I going to nudge this brute into place? I'm tired. I'll worry about it tomorrow. I feel like a water-logged French Scarlett O'Hara. I guess M. Teurnier is my Rhett Butler, and in his own way has just told me "I don't give a damn."

CHAPTER III

The Cutting Edge

THE NEXT DAY I come with a shovel, a pickax and a large bucket; it's one of the buckets we used to scrape all the "gook" out of the lower boat. I've borrowed a pair of hip-high boots from my friend and painting buddy, Jo Lancaster. I also have a winch, what the French call a *tire-fort*, along with two significant lengths of chain that were part of the mooring system for the old wooden boat.

I use the plank, M. Teurnier's plank, to walk across to the boat. I walk along the narrow passage beside the upper boat to the bollard. I loop my short chain over it, then hook one end of my winch to both ends of rope. I throw the rest of the winch onto the bank. I know damned well everything I'm going to do would drive a real boatperson amok. This will be strictly a landlubber's solution. But, after all, that's what I am.

Next, I go straighten out my winch, wrap the longer of its two chains around the largest tree on the bank, bring it down and attach both ends to the hook on the other end of the winch. I begin cranking to take up any slack. I'll be trying the impossible, digging a channel through the sand barge with my shovel into which I can pull my canted boat against the shore. This is all according to my general life-theory that if you don't know how things *should* be done, everything is possible.

I wade into the water in Jo's hip boots, carrying the shovel. I decide I probably won't need the bucket. I'll just throw the sand farther out into the river. I'm wishing I had Matt with me to crank the winch as I dig. I start digging. The boat looms above me. I dig under the rear end of the boat on the land side, where it's grounded. Each time I think I've cleared it a smidgen, I give a few cranks on the winch. I can't tell if it's working or not. A few passersby are convinced I've completely lost my marbles. It goes slowly, but I can actually see the boat is inching its way closer to shore. I check to see if the cables I've strung holding the front of the barge are secure enough.

They're fine. I'm back in the water. I'm working out the hang of it. Thank God, that sandbar is sand, so most of what I scoop into my shovel, I can actually throw out of the way, deeper into the river. If it were mud, as most of the bottom here is, it'd be hopeless.

Just then, the beat-up *deux chevaux* arrives. It's one of *les frères Teurnier,* the one who dressed M. Jacques Teurnier in his diving suit. He stares at me a few minutes, trying to figure it out, then begins to laugh. It's as if he's crept up on someone building a pyramid with pebbles. I admit I'm beginning to have great sympathy for those Egyptian slaves working in the shadow of pyramids hanging over them, stacking gigantic blocks while they weren't even sure if the whole uncanny-looking mess wasn't going to topple over on them.

When he's finished laughing, he begins hauling out more equipment. I'm still puzzled about how he's going to cut out the windows, we can't even get *into* the bottom boat now. I have only a very small plastic dinghy without any oars from which he can work. It came with the wooden boat. He looks around, shrugs. I'm wishing I had Matt to translate. He makes movements as if he's rowing a boat. *I* shrug. He holds up a finger and goes downriver along the *chemin de halage* past the Le Clerc boat. I go back to my digging in the river.

The next thing I know, he's rowing a huge metal rowboat laboriously upriver. He pulls it close to the barge, where it's been cut off and where I'm still digging. I'll never know how he conjured up this monstrosity of a rowboat, but it's perfect for the job. He edges close to shore and indicates I'm to pass the equipment he's unloaded onto the bank into the boat.

This proves to be just barely within my capacity. These river men must be strong as gorillas. And I'm amazed at the number of tools, from gas tanks to red electrical boxes, that are needed.

When I have all the equipment passed on and am ready to pass out myself, he muscles his way up onto the deck of the barge, then hands down the equipment that's up there. He gives me a sign to wait, and walks along the plank onto the *berge*. He climbs up and pulls from his car coils of heavy electrical wire. I watch as he plugs this wire into the mains of the wooden boat, uncoils it toward us along the apron of the metal barge and leads it down to where I've been digging.

After checking to see if the equipment is working, he motions me to join him in his rowboat. I can just struggle myself up the side and fall to the bottom. He hands me a piece of blue chalk and makes a motion with his arm for me to indicate where I want the back window cut. We're cutting this window into the sliced-off end of the barge. I've no idea of what I want; I'm working blind. Practically at random, I mark out about where I'd like a big window cut from the bulkhead.

He hands me a helmet with thick glasses and indicates I should put it on my head. I do this. Now we're astronauts about ready to take a space walk. He shows me how to keep the wires and tubes from tangling, at the same time holding the rowboat tight close to the barge. Practically without warning, he then starts to cut through the metal with a huge spinning disk. A shower of sparks fly like fireworks, bouncing against him, me and the boat, giant sparklers on the Fourth of July. He's resolutely cutting through the metal, right along the blue chalk line I made so casually. I'm hoping the lines are square, but he seems to have a level and rule built into his mind. In half an hour, he has the entire rectangle cut out, except for a small corner on the river side. It's about two meters wide and a meter high.

He lifts his helmet and goggles, then hand-signals the question, smiling, shrugging. He wants to know where he should put the piece he's about finished cutting. I shrug back, my French is improving. He points down into the river just below where he's been cutting. I nod OK. What else?

He leaves everything in the boat, including me, and runs up to his car. He scrambles back with what looks like a giant's crowbar. With this, he angles the huge metal rectangle he's made away from the back of the boat, prying it out. He motions for me to climb out of the boat. I do this with no misgivings. He then pushes the rowboat away from the barge a half meter and gives one more quick flashing cut with his revolving wheel. That immense plate of solid steel drops into the water like a knife. I watch as it settles to the bottom. He smiles, pushes his helmet and goggles back. I smile, I don't know why. I wonder how this chunk of steel imbedded in the sandbar is going to affect my digging operation.

Let There Be Light!

Now, from the same power line, he rigs an electric light and passes it into the hull of the boat. He points at his feet, and I realize I should change from these high hip boots to my smaller boots in the upper boat. Using the same plank he did, I manage to muscle my way up there. God, it's a mess. When I come back, he has all the cutting equipment inside the barge. He's also digging on the bank with my shovel and filling the bucket with wet river sand. He walks the plank to the upper boat with bucket in hand, and motions me into the lower boat. I make my awkward scrabble into the rowboat. I'm losing all pride. He lowers the bucket of sand from the deck of the upper boat down to me. It must weigh much less up there than it does down where I am, because I almost drop the whole thing and have a hard time keeping my balance.

I lean the bucket on the bottom ledge of the ragged, sharp-cut hole. He's already lowering himself, like an acrobat, from the barge down to the rowboat, a rowboat I could probably never even row. He eases himself through the newly cut window, pointing out to me the sharpness of the edges, and that I'm to come in with him. Luckily, I'm wearing the gloves I wore while shoveling away my sandbar. In comparison, that little escapade begins to look like fun and games.

Inside, he's hung the light. He has a welding torch and the tanks set up on the floor. Together, we haul the acetylene and oxygen tanks down from his *deux chevaux* into the rowboat and then into the barge. I can feel my back wanting to slip right out of my body; I tighten my butt.

When we're all ready, he wants to know where I want the windows cut. I try to remember Teurnier's instructions. I take the blue chalk, and, in the semidark, without being able to see where the water line *really* is on the outside, I start marking windows at least a meter apart, not more than a meter wide each, and, hopefully, at least a half meter above water level. I keep peeking out the back window to make an approximation and pray we don't sink this boat.

He points out how I'm to stay beside him while wearing my helmet and glasses. He pantomimes clearly that if a spark lights the oil around us, we could burn or explode, so I'm to throw sand on it immediately. I wonder if this is standard procedure or if he's just some kind of sadist who enjoys watching the American turn white.

It's amazing how fast he cuts out the windows. I mark between times as he cuts away. I mark four windows on the land side. I'm hoping to have six on the river side, making eleven windows in all, counting the one in back. I have no idea how I'm going to use all this space in the hull, but I know I want less visibility from the bank and more vistas looking over the river.

By some magic, probably his experience, we come out with the bottoms of the windows about sixty centimeters above water level. It's a strange feeling because, looking out, the water level is about knee-height inside. But there is some light now.

A Taste of Real Work

We work all day long. Luckily we're cutting out the windows, because the smell of acetylene is almost unbearable. Three different times, small fires break out in the oil on the floor of the boat. Twice, I can stamp them out, but once it gets big enough so I need to throw some of the sand from my bucket over the spot.

By asking Gaston, the brother Teurnier who's doing the cutting, I find out how to do things. I keep thinking of just saying, "After you, Gaston," then climbing through one of the windows and walking away. I never realized how soft and unprepared for hard labor I am. So far, this boat has been teaching me some lessons concerning truly hard work and humility.

For one thing, it's dangerous, whether it's bringing up a sunken boat, cleaning out the oil muck, floating a boat down the river, pumping madly while sliding one boat on top of another as it's trying its best to tip, digging in the river with boots up to my armpits, or this, cutting out panels of metal with an acetylene torch.

When I'd taken on the task of rebuilding the wooden boat before it sunk, I thought *that* was hard work. To these people it was mere child's play, not to be compared with *real* work. So far, as well as knocking about five years off my life, if I get to *live* five more, this whole boat experience is worth it.

First, Gaston hands out his gloves, goggles, mask and helmet. Then he muscles up one of the supposedly empty tanks, slides it over the edge of the window, and I lower it into the bottom of the rowboat. The boat tips and I just about fall out. It's dark enough so that, with the tipping boat and my oily, slippery boots, I almost take a header into the river. Gaston laughs. It must look ridiculous to him watching a grown man staggering around in what for him is a steady rowboat.

When we have everything out, he practically vaults through the window, lands like a big tomcat in the rowboat, picks up one oar and pushes us off from the big boat toward the shore. All the windows on the land side are cut out in this back section, and it begins to resemble, vaguely, some kind of boat for cruising in the Mediterranean—very vaguely, that is.

We wrestle the tanks onto the shore. I push them toward him from the boat until he manages a good hold, then he drags them, slipping as he goes, in the dark, up to the battered Citroën. Last, I hand him his goggles, helmet, mask and gloves. He reaches out to give me a hand so I can make the jump from boat to shore. I'm feeling like a real lummox, clumsy and dumb.

We beat our way through the nettles and muddy bank up to his car. I try to help him load the bottles into the car, probably more in the way than anything. He's smiling. His entire face, except where his goggles and mask have protected him, is black.

He gives me a pat on the shoulder, almost breaking my scapula, and holds up seven fingers, then points at the boat. He says, *"Demain, à sept heures?"* I nod. He climbs into his 2CV and starts backing up, at high speed, down the *chemin de halage.* I stand watching him, holding my hand out almost as if I'm giving a Hitler salute. My kids have already warned me against waving to an adult Frenchman—only children do that. They just hold out a hand. He's looking over his shoulder to back out and doesn't even see me.

I look down at the boat with its four blank eyes and think of tomorrow. Is there any way I can just drop this whole thing? Nope, I'm in too deep. That isn't an appropriate comment when you're dealing with boats, at least the kind of boats I seem to have.

A Temporary Retreat

My car is up in the village on the street. I'm covered with oil, mud and sweat. I tuck clean clothes from the car under my arm and go to the local café, order a beer as my excuse, then go into the toilet, a squatter, undress and redress hurriedly. I turn the jeans inside out and roll the filthy boots inside the jeans along with the sweaty shirts. I pull on ordinary clothes.

There's a small sink with cold water, and I do the best I can with my face and hands. I'll need white spirits to clean off this mess.

When I come out, my beer is flat but I drink it. I've been thirsty all day and almost didn't notice. I pay. Now it's completely dark. I phone home to say I'll be there in about an hour. The traffic should hold me up that long. I tell Rosemary to go ahead and eat with the kids, just save something for me. She's very sympathetic, wants to know what's happened. I say I'll tell her later, but that I'm all right.

CHAPTER IV

In the Hands of the Gods

THE NEXT DAY, I'm out of the apartment by six and on the site before seven, but Gaston is already there and sliding the tanks down the bank. I give him a hand, and we work it through the window again and set up. I'm stiff from yesterday but find this easier than I thought it would be. Little do I know.

Gaston indicates to me with wonderful pantomime (the skill must run in the family) that we're going to cut the entire wall running along the length of the boat, leaving only the triangular supports that hold up the deck, and now, *in addition,* the weight of my wooden, original boat. To me it seems like an impossible task. For example, what are we going to do with the huge slab of solid steel he's proposing to cut out? We can't just slip it through a window; it's too big. It's all in the hands of the gods—and Gaston.

The way he does it, and with incredible speed, is to cut out small panels, ceiling to floor, about three feet wide, panels we can push through the riverside window. He first cuts a doorway through and lets that panel, about three feet by six, drop onto the steel ribs supporting the hull of the boat. It makes a tremendous clang.

Grunting, we then move this over to the dark side, the river side. Gaston insists we shove it right against the wall, but flat. He doesn't seem to have any intention of pushing it out the window after all.

Then, he moves the light into the next section. He now has a nonoiled platform, the first section he cut out, on which to stand and work. From it, he cuts out a window facing onto the river. We push it out as before and watch as it drops out of sight through the murky depths and into the mud at the bottom of the river.

He goes along like this, cutting about three feet at a time from the center-wall divider, letting each heavy piece of metal drop to the floor so we can stick it to the outside edge of the boat and stand on it. Then he moves his equipment onto the new platform and cuts another window. I'm figuring and running along, chalking on this riverside wall where the windows should be. I'm also wondering how I'm going to close them in again. How does one attach glass to metal? Is there some special kind of magic metal glue?

But it's nice having air blow through. We go along the back half of the boat like that, cutting two more windows, each a meter wide and spaced a meter apart. Now we're up to the bulkhead dividing the front part of the boat from the back. He indicates with his arms where he wants me to mark out the parts of the bulkhead to be cut out as doors. I decide I'll have two double doors cut through, one on each side of the central divider, rather than try to cut out the entire bulkhead. I'm still concerned about the weight on the upper-boat deck, and here we are undercutting the whole structure.

So I mark the spaces to be cut, each large enough for a double door. He looks, nods and begins burning away. Before lunch, those two holes are cut, and I see for the first time the enormity of the boat, its entire length. From inside, it looks even larger than it did from outside.

I suggest we go to lunch. I'm a nervous wreck, anything to get out of this hell of a hull for a little while. He looks at me and down at himself. Naturally, I've put on my work clothes again, and he's filthy as before. I explain it's a *routier* place, and he smiles. We leave everything in place, except we haul up the two big bottles of gas. We've about used them up again. We slide them into the 2CV.

Gaston and I, between the two of us, as well as putting down a full meal, *routier*-style, tuck in a liter of wine. I'm somewhat worried because, for every glass I drink, he drinks two. But then I shouldn't have worried: Gaston is French-Breton, and three-quarters of a bottle of wine is just warming up.

After lunch, we first go to a supply place that's practically covered with weeds and rusty gas tanks. This is where we turn in the empty bottles and pick up two new filled ones. I'm helping carry these brutes to the car and trying to forget about my bad back. There's no time for anything like a mere sore back.

When we come back to the boat again, Gaston decides to start cutting out the center wall of the next two sections, that is, the front two. He indicates I'm to continue keeping an eye out for any fires, with the sand nearby. Also, I begin to mark the places where I want these windows. I measure more carefully and place two on the land side and three on the river side. As he cuts each section of the wall out, I lean down and give him a hand moving it over toward the windows, but this time on the land side of the boat.

Again he uses these metal panels as standing platforms for cutting out windows. He's working at a furious pace, cutting, burning, dropping the panels like cards in a deck.

Now I begin to see the boat as a place I might develop. I keep stepping back at different angles to have some perspective. I feel my spirits coming up; just as each of those boats did, I feel myself coming to the surface.

We finish before it's dark. I try to give Gaston some money, but he makes it clear he's already been paid. This took some pantomime, but we manage. He won't take any extra money for a drink either. We've worked the gas bottles back to his car, and he's in a hurry to go home. He probably has a family and didn't get home until after nine or ten last night. We agree to come back to work Monday morning. I'm not learning much French, but before long I'll be giving pantomime like Marcel Marceau.

A Quick Visit, Then Back to the Grind

The next day is Saturday, so I bring Rosemary and the kids out to see what we've done. They're all impressed. Everybody's starting to divide up the different sections as to where they're going to sleep. I don't tell them how far in the future that will be, if ever.

Gaston has taken the rowboat back to wherever he found it, so we push our way out in the little plastic dinghy that came with the original boat. We put an old army blanket over the sharp edges so everyone can climb in through the window. Even Rosemary manages the maneuver. Matt, with his broken ankle, makes it, too. We all have on boots or old shoes. It's fun wandering around in the blackness of the hold with just the light punctuation from the windows we've cut. It seems almost blacker now than it was without the windows. That's blacker, not darker.

I'm worried how I'm going to work out a way going from the upper boat down to the lower one and vice versa. This will be a good problem. I locate from an interior oil spout exactly where the hatches have been cut on the deck of the metal boat and then try to estimate where they'd come out in relation to the upper boat. I want the stairway to come down from what had been the entry room, where our youngest, Camille, might sleep. I'll need to do some careful measuring, and then it will mostly be by guess and by God and by Gaston, more hit and miss than anything, hopefully more hit than miss.

On Monday, we go right to work. Gaston has already brought the bottles down and is lighting the torch. He starts to finish off the long center divider he was working on Friday. Then he moves over and begins on the windows I've marked. He's finished by noon. He's in even more of a hurry than before. When the last window makes its sharklike slide into the water, he looks around, shrugs to see if there's anything else I want cut out. I point to the hatch opening I'm hoping to use as a way down from the upper boat.

With no qualms, he prepares to cut it out. It's over his head, so I signal "wait," dash out the window on the plank to the *berge,* up the rickety gangplank into the wooden boat and grab the one chair that for some reason didn't fall apart too badly. I've glued it as best I can. I retrace my route and bring it in to him. He checks it for steadiness. He's already marked with blue chalk where he intends to cut through. I nod my head and smile.

Then he starts. It's much more hellish than cutting on the side. The sparks and bits of hot metal drop onto his helmet and mask. He's also taken a neckerchief from his back pocket and wrapped it around his mouth and nose. Every few minutes, he lowers his arms. That torch must be deadly heavy. There's nothing I can do except watch and wonder. One thing I'm wondering is why he doesn't cut from the upper boat.

But he manages. He cuts out an additional foot to the hatch, which makes it about five feet long. He then motions me to go upstairs, just over him. I make the same running, sliding, jumping, climbing, across-the-gangplank maneuver, and when I get there, he's already burned a hole through the wooden hull and upper floor. It's within six inches of where I'd hoped it would be. Of course, the deck is on fire. I stamp it out, feeling like the boy who stood on the burning deck, but I'm no boy! He burns another hole so now we can see each other. I stamp this fire out, too.

All by hand motions, I show him where I want the hole cut through the wooden bottom of the upper boat. I've gone into the kitchen and filled a muddy pot with water, with which I keep dousing the flames, trying not to pour too much water on Gaston.

And, believe it or not, he cuts the entire hole out that way. This part is solid oak and would have taken days to cut with a handsaw. I make sure all the charred wood is wet, the fires out, then run down into the hull again. He's putting his things together. I help him with the hoses and tanks. He points to his watch and makes a sign to me pumping his fist in the air. I figure it out. He's in a hurry.

We push, roll, slide the tanks and equipment up to his 2CV. When he closes the back doors, he takes a minute to look down at the boat, the windows. We can see through to the other side now. He smiles. I'm smiling, too. I can't believe he did it. He puts out his hand and we shake. He looks at his watch again. I imagine he has some other job to do this afternoon, maybe some other fool with an impossible task.

He'll probably eat the sack lunch he has on the front seat of his *deux chevaux*. I don't know, I'm only guessing. I've already brought out my wallet and tried to give him money again, but he pushes me off. And when he pushes, he really pushes; I almost fall over. I watch him roar down the *chemin de halage* backward. He turns at the boathouse and he's gone.

CHAPTER V

Getting Up in the World—and Down

I'M DEAD POOPED again, mostly from sheer nervousness. I didn't actually do that much, but it's all so fast, beyond my control. I sit on the bank staring at my boat, or boats. I slide down and winch in the boat another few inches, then go down inside the wooden boat and look through the hole he's just cut. I try figuring how I'll build the staircase. The first thing I'll need will be a ladder. I know a place in the next town, called Le Pecq, where I can most likely find one.

First, because the hardware store won't be open yet, I go across the street to that café Sisley painted all those years ago, in 1876. I order a *jambon beurre*—a ham sandwich with butter on half a baguette. I order a beer with it and try settling down, both physically and mentally. I start trying to figure how to estimate the angle and length of the staircase. It's a nice little problem in geometry, except I don't know all the measurements; but I can come up with some idea. I have a pencil and paper as well as a tape measure in the trunk of the car.

I pay my bill, walk over to my car to check what tools I actually have, then start off for Le Pecq. No matter, I'm definitely going to need a ladder. Climbing in and out of my window from the little plastic bobbing dinghy, or that big humping beast Gaston borrowed from somewhere, would just be asking for trouble.

I calculate the height from floor to ceiling to be about eight feet at that spot. The top of the metal boat curves up slightly there toward the bow, so it's generally higher inside. If I can find a three-, or better yet, a four-meter ladder, it should do. This is going to burn another hole in my pocketbook.

The hardware store has just opened when I arrive. I'm their first customer for the afternoon. I explain what I want by imitating a man climbing a ladder. The woman at the counter motions me to follow her. This hardware store is like a warren, a series of houses and courtyards joined together. We weave our way through it all, and she shows me a big drum with heavy rope.

My pantomime wasn't as good as the Teurniers', but I spot some ladders at the back of the store. I point, she smiles and imitates my motions for climbing a ladder, shakes her head, then does a much more effective simulation, impossible to confuse her interpretation with rope climbing. I imagine the French are naturally good at mime.

I buy a five-meter aluminum ladder and she gives me some rope to tie it on the roof. She also rips off a piece of red paper from a box and pantomimes tying it to the end of the ladder. I smile and take it along with the bill. I may be getting up in the world, but I'm down in the pocketbook.

I'm careful going out with the ladder, watching front and back so I don't wipe anybody out. I've seen too many Laurel and Hardy movies. I make it to the car about a block away. I have a minimum rack on my minimum car, and when I tie the ladder onto it, even with the front of the ladder sticking way forward over the hood, the back end sticks out almost another two meters. I tie my piece of red paper onto the end. If some cop in a bad mood sees me, I'm in trouble. But what else is there to do? And this is only the beginning!

But, by some miracle I do make it to the boat OK. I climb the hanging old broken gangplank into the upper boat with the idea of lowering my ladder into the hold, but there's not enough clearance. I need to go through the window on the plank again, only holding a ladder this time. It's getting worse and worse. Finally, I do something smart. I lean the ladder on the bank and swing it out onto the lip of the window. Then I monkey-crawl along it into the boat. I pull the ladder in behind me. I consider this brainstorm a good omen.

The ladder is just the right length. Now I have reasonable access to the lower boat from the upper, so I go up and back down a few times. I've been singing an old song, one my father used to sing, which goes: "Close the doors, they're coming through the windows, close the windows, they're coming through the doors." I don't remember any of the other words, so I find myself singing that ditty over and over again with gusto. The metal boat has great acoustics.

I've brought along with me in my back pocket the rope with which I tied the ladder onto the car roof. Another good omen. I didn't think of it or plan it, but I take the advantage. I tie the rope to a nail sticking out from the burned-through boat bottom. I lower myself down the ladder, letting out the rope as I go. I keep walking back and forth with the other end of the rope, trying to decide where I want the foot of the ladder to be. At the same time, I'm estimating the angle that will minimize the steepness and still allow a person with reasonable acrobatic ability, and a bit of ducking, to come down through the passage between decks.

No matter what, with this hole and this angle, I'm going to have both problems, a steep, almost ladderlike staircase on which one will need to do a quick duck.

Building the Ladder of Success

This is before I think of the big problem. Where am I going to find two heavy beams of wood long enough to match the length of my string. It turns out I'll need boards four meters long (that's about thirteen feet). I estimate I can just about make it work with twenty-centimeter steps. I measure the angle and distance over and over again, but that's what it comes to. I consider a spiral staircase, but I could never figure that out, and buying one would cost as much as the whole boat.

So I crawl out on my ladder again and go down to a large building materials place at the end of our village. Most of the wood they have is for constructing roofs of buildings. I drive my car in, park and start wandering around with my tape measure, searching for boards that are long enough. It's an immense, open yard.

When I'm about to give up, a worker, probably Portuguese, not French, strolls over to me. I try telling him what I want. Luckily, I know the numbers better than most words and I know meters. He motions me to follow him. We go into another shed and there they are, roof beams. He points out the four-meter ones. They're about three inches by ten inches, *serious*! I show him with my fingers "two" and say *"deux."* He shakes his hand at the wrist in the usual motion to indicate expensive in any Latin country. When I ask *"Combien?"* he points past my shoulder to the office.

It's a madhouse in there, mostly professional builders. Finally I work my way to the counter. By now, I've drawn out, with one of their pencils, what I want. The clerk starts paging through catalogues with rows of sizes and prices. He holds up his fingers for first four, then two. I nod. He writes down two prices, according to the quality of wood. I choose the lesser one, lesser but not enough less. He starts filling out an invoice. He does all the figuring on an old-time Monroe calculator.

He comes up with a number significantly larger than what I'd expected. I'd forgotten about the TVA, that is, value-added tax. I search deeper in my wallet and have enough, barely enough. I pay. He gives me the invoice and waves me out to the yard. I show the invoice to the first man I'd spoken to, the yard man, and he motions me to bring my car up close. When I pull up in my little Hillman Husky, he almost falls over laughing. I show how I still have rope from my ladder purchase. He makes a movement to indicate the roof will cave in. I convince him I'll take them one at a time. He shrugs, lifts one end of one of the beams and I the other.

He's right. The roof could very easily cave in. We lower it onto the rack, and the rack buckles against the roof of the car. I start tying it in place. He helps. I have the piece of red paper I used for the ladder. I tie it on. I try to get across how I'll be right back for the other beam. He smiles and nods his head. I scrunch as I climb into the car. I can see the headliner is already buckling. Rosemary is going to kill me, she loves this little English car we bought on her sabbatical.

Going slowly, about five miles an hour, I make my way back to the boat. The entire auto is creaking and groaning. I pull up as close to the boat as possible. Then I twist and pull until one end of the board is on the ground. The other end I lower slowly, thinking all the while, "use your knees, keep your head up." I still need to go pick up that second beam, and if my back goes out I'm in big trouble.

I leave the beam at the top of the *berge* on the *chemin de halage.* Nobody's going to run away with it.

I climb back in the car and punch the bent roof back into place from inside. This time I take with me the blanket I'd spread over the window edge to keep from being cut by the sharp metal. I throw it in the car. No use making more scratches and dents in the roof than necessary. Maybe I'll need to sell this car to pay for the boat materials, who knows?

The yard worker seems surprised when I come back. We lift the beam same as before and tie it down. The roof kinks in a little deeper this time. I give the guy ten francs for helping me. That's all I have left.

I creep out of the yard in first gear, carefully going over the

small curb as I slide out, avoiding all the monster trucks pulling up
to the yard with hundreds of sacks of cement There are huge trailer
trucks, piles of lumber, tiles, plywood. It's a regular maze. Next to
them, I look like a mosquito buzzing around water buffalo. But I
do make it down to the boat, where I reenact my unloading scene,
lowering the beam from the roof of the car. This time the roof
pops up on its own.

The old gangplank to the upper boat is completely ripped
up. We took it off when we pulled the wooden boat out to the
marriage with the steel hull. It's filthy with dried river mud, and
I've just barely muscled it to the edge of the water. So, I see, it's the
up-the-ladder-and-through-the-window trick again.

I push the ladder out the window to the bank, climb out on it
and monkey-crawl across it. When I'm up on the deck, I look
down through the hole of the upper boat into the lower boat,
make some mental calculations and realize I'll never be able to
push this stairway down the hole even if I could get the beams up
on deck; there isn't enough clearance. I'll need to go through the
window again and somehow drag the beams back with me. This
turns out to be quite an operation.

I slide one of the beams down the bank using gravity, friction
and my puny strength. I try edging it up onto the sharp sill of a
middle window and almost fall into the river doing it. In fact, I'm
wet with mud and water up to my knees. I do, however, with a last
desperate effort, catch the beam onto the edge of the window. As a
reward, I slide down the bank into the water up to my waist. I sit,
sweating like a pig on my upper parts and shivering on the lower.
I pull myself together, climb out of this acid bath.

After a few minutes rest, I begin edging, pushing, bit by bit,
sliding the beam over the sharp-cut window edge and into the
lower boat. It's about here I realize I could have just slid the beam
over the ladder into the window. But then, I must recognize,
planning ahead isn't my style. I muscle up and push the rest of

the beam in, so about three feet of it is in the boat.

I stand there looking at it, then stare back at the other board up on the edge of the quay. I keep reminding myself that Rome wasn't built in a day; at this point I'm surprised anything has ever gotten built anywhere.

But I slog up the hill again and do the same dragging and hauling of the other beam down to the edge of the water. My intention is to slide this beam on top of the first, thus not have the miseries I've just survived. After some considerable struggling to keep the second board lined up on the first one, this works out fine. I give a few more cranks on the winch, pulling the back end of the boat closer to shore. I've discovered that by some kind of river magic, just leaving the boat sit there alone, even without my feverish shoveling, seems to wash away the sandbar and, so, bit by bit, I've been able to pull that end of the boat closer in to where I want it. Also, I find I can slide the top beam into the boat. The bottom beam is tougher because it's caught on the rough edges of the window, but I manage. Now for some brain work as well as brawn. First I take a little rest.

I scramble up the bank onto the *chemin de halage*. There's a smiling, well-built man standing there watching me. He puts out his hand to shake. My hands aren't too filthy, so I take his hand. It turns out he runs a little restaurant just across the Rue de Paris, the main drag through Port Marly. He and his wife run it. His wife cooks and he serves. They have one son. As soon as he catches on to the low quality of my French, he slows his down and enunciates so I can understand. I guess running a restaurant you learn to do that.

We have a nice chat. He tells me he's been watching me with my struggle. He's a black-belt judo instructor and gives lessons to the kids in the village. Most guys I know who do that kind of stuff are hard-nosed, martial arts and all that, but this fellow is real laid-back, easy to talk to.

He says he's been coming over once in a while to watch me,

and it's much to be doing by myself. He volunteers to come give a hand if I ever find myself with something I can't handle. That's what I call neighborly. But I'm ready to face up to the beams again. We shake and I slide down the *berge*.

The Battle of the Beams

But first the battle with the beams. I drag one through the window, bouncing over the support struts in the bottom of the boat, to the base of the ladder I've put in place leading to the upper boat. Then, rung by rung, I advance one end of this heavy brute up the aluminum ladder, the ladder I should have been using all along, until we reach the top and can lean the beam at the edge of the cut to the upper boat. I climb down the ladder and, midway, reaching out, manage to twist the beam so it's sitting up on the narrow side. The angle doesn't look too bad, but it doesn't exactly look like a staircase either, more like a large, awkward half of a wooden ladder.

I pull the other beam into place the same way. I try lining them up. I do this by eye. It's about here when I'm in the upper boat, lining things up, that I accidentally bump the ladder so it slides and falls into the bottom boat. Now I have no way to get either out to the lower boat or down from the upper boat. I've figuratively painted myself into a corner. It's the kind of situation I seem to find myself in too often.

Risers, Steps, a Tug-of-War and Dreams of Canaries

Then, I remember the winch at the back of the boat. I gingerly work my way along the two-foot-wide overlap of the metal boat from under the wooden boat and come to the winch. It consists of two rather thin cables attached to a ratchet and pulley. I'm wearing gloves and as there's nothing else to do, I lower myself over the edge of the upper boat and, hand over hand, waggle myself onto land. I give the winch an extra crank while I'm at it. The back end of the boat is now only about two feet from where I want it to be.

I sit on the bank, still wet, top and bottom, and try to figure some easier way to climb back on my boat than hanging by the winch. I bring the rope down from the car, tie one end of it onto the old gangplank and throw the rope in a loop, sort of a poor man's cowboy lasso and finally, after about fifty throws, manage to hook it onto one of the bollards and fish the other end of the rope out of the water.

Now I have a tug-of-war on my hands. It's me against the boat. But I finally do it and shimmy up onto the deck, tying the old gangplank more or less firmly in place so I can gingerly descend by it if necessary. I walk into the upper boat and look down the hole at my ladder. Now, how do I get down there? I'm still stuck. I've got to master this staircase soon or I'm going to go completely bananas.

I actually slide down one of those planks, picking up three monster splinters in scattered parts of my body, but I retrieve the ladder.

Now it's time to measure. I start marking with a rule and pencil the locations for the stairs. I redo it about three times before it comes out right, that is, so ordinary people, not just kangaroos, can climb to the top or lower themselves into the lower boat.

With this thought, I call it a day and drive home.

Chapter VI

White as Driven Snow

I'M NOT ABOUT to try explaining to the family what I've been doing. On the way home, I start dreaming again about having an aviary for canaries on the back two meters of the protruding lower-boat deck. I could lean out the back bedroom window of the upper boat and feed them. I'd build it with double mesh to keep away cats. I've had large canary aviaries in the past, but what with living in a small apartment here in Paris haven't had much chance lately. It would be great.

Over the next two days, I spend all my time building the staircase. First I buy more wood at the building-and-supply place. This wood is lighter weight than what I bought as the main braces for the sides. I've brought out my tools from Paris, both hand and power. I'm not really a "tool man." I inherited the hand tools from my dad, who had spent part of his life as a carpenter, and since then I've accumulated a Skil saw, a power drill, and a jigsaw. It isn't much to tackle a job like this, but I feel ready after yesterday's fiasco.

The first thing is to cut the bottom of the beams so they line up with each other and, more than that, will be sitting flat on the floor, that is, *when* I lay the floor. I use the simple geometric laws about complementary and supplementary angles, and mark the cut. Of course, I don't really believe it until my eye sees this has to be the correct angle. And believe it or not, it turns out to be about right. Sometimes method does pay off.

I cut the stairs and make braces for under each step. I drill holes to screw in the braces, so as not to split the wood, then drive ten-centimeter screws into these holes. The smell of wood and sawdust is a comfort after the unmitigated smell of oil. It's such a delight to feel more or less in control of what I'm doing, too.

When I finish screwing in the last step, I practice going up and down a few times. Going up is easy. I just lean forward and if I want, climb on all fours, but it isn't necessary. Coming down is harder. I find it best to go the first four steps facing down, then, as my shoulders come to the cut between the two boats, I turn and go the rest of the way backward, the way one would on a ladder. It isn't perfect, but it's good enough for me.

I've been doing all this work alone because school has started and the rest of the family is busy. I'm about ready now to deal with the floor. I decide first to put in Styrofoam over the oil between the struts, which are set fifty centimeters apart. I'll use Styrofoam three centimeters thick. I do the calculations and go back again to the supply house. It turns out they sell the Styrofoam in panels two-meters-fifty by one-meter-twenty. It also is sold at this place only in packets of ten. A quick guess from my figures shows I'll need at least two packets.

They're getting to know me in the office, and I'm waited on quickly. I've been passing myself off as a professional, but that has to be one of the most transparent lies I've ever tried to pull. They don't care. It's just that I need to pay the TVA and can't recuperate it. I'm learning. I'm spending money so fast I can see us opening up the boat as a poorhouse boat, just for our family.

The Styrofoam is light but very bulky. I take one package at a time on top of the car and quickly discover that almost no matter how slowly I go, the stuff wants to take off, fly away on its own. It keeps fluttering over my eyes out the windshield like butterfly wings. The second load I tie down more carefully. The supply-house people are very generous about giving me all the string-fiber rope I need. I think they're beginning to wonder what the hell I'm going to do with all the Styrofoam.

The next part is easy, too. I cut the Styrofoam with an ordinary kitchen knife and before long, I don't need to measure but can cut it right in place. Having the floor all white makes the entire lower boat seem much lighter, so much so, I figure I'll line the walls with the stuff. It'll be good for insulation, too.

I buy another two bundles and start cutting them to fit between the side bracings of the boat. At first, I try gluing them to the walls, but no glue or mastic I find will stick to the seventy-some years worth of oil that is soaked into those walls, so I learn to cut each section about one-eighth-inch wider than I need, then jam it into place. It works fine.

Of course, now the oil-soaked ceiling looks terrible in comparison, so back I go again and buy two more packs. I use the same squeeze-in system to fit these panels. But I find they want to fall down almost as fast as I put them up, even when I increase the amount of extra width. So I buy a packet of lath and, cutting them a fraction of a centimeter longer, I wedge them sideways in under the ceiling pieces of Styrofoam, and that holds things together.

After about a week's work, it all looks white and beautiful. A surgeon could operate down here if he were a damned fool and romantic enough. I walk on the struts and try not to step on the floors, although it doesn't matter. The Styrofoam is mostly for insulation, not for beauty. But I like the way it takes so much of the oil curse off the boat. I even begin to feel the oil smell isn't as bad.

CHAPTER VII

The Floor Plan

SATURDAY, I ORDER the wood to floor the boat. First I buy pieces like American two-by-fours to lay across the struts so they run along the length of the boat. I try drilling into the struts to hold them in place, but that's impossible. The steel is as hard as, well—steel. I break three specially tempered metal bits trying.

After much worrying at it, I finally realize I only need to place the lengths crosswise to the metal beams, fifty centimeters apart. I mark their location on the metal struts with the same blue chalk I used to mark in the windows. I calculate I'm going to need twenty (the length of the boat) by five (the width of the boat) by two (the number of boards for each meter of width). This comes to two hundred meters of board. I drive down and order this, haul it back in several loads on top of my car. I carry them down the bank and push them through the window. It doesn't take long to position them on the struts.

The next part is easy but expensive. I calculate the number of square meters I'll need to floor this lower boat. It's twenty by five meters, or 100 square meters. I go back to the building supply outfit and start looking around for the least expensive wood that will do the job. After almost giving up, I find some wood long enough, five meters, and cheap enough. It's wood used to make shipping crates and is called *bois de chauffage*. It's unmilled and comes in random lengths and widths. I'm getting into big bucks now.

Thanks to one of my best buyers, I've sold four paintings this past week, so I have the money. I also buy five kilos of number-six, or six-centimeter, nails. This is long enough to go through the floorboards, then through the depth of the wood I'm calling floor joists. I'm glad my dad isn't here to see the crazy way I'm doing this job.

I ask about delivery costs and time of delivery for the flooring wood, then decide I can do it myself, definitely quicker and cheaper. I spend the better part of the next day hauling this wood back to the boat.

The men working in the yard are nice enough to let me go through the stacks and choose the best boards. I try to avoid large knots that might fall out, or pieces that are really rough and unfinished. When I've made my choices and set them aside, they make quite a pile. The average width of the boards is about eight inches.

I put the poor Hillman to the test again. I find I can take five boards at a time. I'm getting a real workout pressing those five-meter boards up on top of the car, tying them down, then unloading them and piling them on the *chemin de halage*. The boards hang over the front and back of the car more than the length of the Hillman itself. I hate to think what Rosemary would say if she saw me misusing her lovely automobile so ruthlessly.

There are over eighty boards, so that means sixteen trips. I lose count after about the seventh load. I'm thinking about Camus and *The Myth of Sisyphus*. Just as it's getting dark, I unload the last boards. I consider moving them all down to the edge of the water for safety, but I'm too tired. I push in three boards through the window and climb in over them. I want to test my theory as to how this is going to work. I start at the back of the boat, the flat end where we cut out the first window. The boards fit lengthwise perfectly from one side of the boat to the other. I don't have to cut anything off there. Up in the bow of the boat, it narrows, and I'll need to cut to shape.

I jam the boards into place before nailing anything, checking to see that the joists are still lined up, then get out my hammer and nails. I go along pounding in nails and hoping for the best. My theory is to let gravity help me keep all this in place. By pushing the boards tight against each other and nailing into the joists, nothing can move. It's all held by the weight of the floor itself. I put three nails in at each joist, or thirty nails across each board. In all, I drive ninety nails in, three boards. When it's wide enough so I can stand, it's solid as I could ever wish.

It's getting too dark to work, so I quit, leaving the hammer and box of nails just where I finished. I know now I'm going to need help, as my arm is about to fall off. I can nail reasonably well, but enough is enough. I figure on organizing a big nailing party next Saturday.

The Nailing Party

When I park the car and go up to the apartment, I make my announcement. Matt's willing; he has his cast off and is walking around fine. He'll do his weekend homework tonight. Rosemary says she doesn't think she can help with the nailing, but there has to be something she can do. There sure is.

We work out a list of friends we think might be willing or able to give us a hand. After about ten phone calls, I have three volunteers. We're going to make a sort of picnic out of it, potluck. The crew will be, besides myself: Matt, Robin and Donna Cody, Neil and Barbara Austin, plus my painting buddy, Jo Lancaster. Most of them teach at the same school as Rosemary.

We agree to meet at the boat by nine o'clock. Robin and Neil say they'll be there. We, that is, my family, take off from Paris at seven-thirty. We can beat most of the traffic that way. When we arrive, Robin and Donna are already there, Robin with hammer in hand, a good Stanley. Donna has a big pot of spaghetti and one of her outstanding rhubarb pies.

It's a beautiful day, a real Indian summer day. The leaves from the maples and willows on the bank are falling like snow from the slight frost the night before. I take everybody up the old gang-plank, then down the new stairs to see how it looks. It almost looks like new construction with just the white, and now, at the far end, those few boards I've nailed in place.

Just then, Neil and Barbara Austin arrive. She's carrying a monster tray filled with lasagna. Luckily, the upper boat still has the butane stove working so we can heat these goodies up before we eat. Next comes Jo Lancaster, and he has four bottles of wine and two hammers.

"Three red for the he-men and one white for the fish course."

We start carrying down the boards and pushing them through the windows. The women are a big help with this. When we have enough boards down, we push several boards in place. Now we have a real platform from which to nail. We space ourselves, dis-tribute nails and start pounding. The only rule is no pounding down bent nails. Either they go in straight or they have to be broken off or pulled out. Actually, the wood is reasonably soft and easy to nail. How I'd love to have some real oak. Hard to nail, but it would be beautiful.

By lunch, we're about halfway done. I'm beginning to worry about the nails lasting. The supply house is closed on Saturdays. I consider changing from three nails for each joist to two. If we do that, we can probably make it.

We set out the lunch on the table I've glued back together and cleaned off. We buy three baguettes, and the women have set things up so we serve ourselves. Most of us pull chairs out onto the *chemin de halage*. This old path the donkeys used to pull the barges up to the locks has been converted by us into a picnic ground. It's beautiful with the yellow and red leaves all around us in the sunshine.

It's Robin who, between bites of lasagna, brings us the inevitable question.

"Will, what in heaven's name are you doing here with this boat? It can't go anywhere. You're working yourself to a frazzle, we never see you around anymore. The smell of the river is like a sewer and the inside of the boat smells like death itself."

"Robin, it's a question I've been asking myself since I got involved with this. At first, I was sure it was all some kind of nightmare accident and would disappear when I woke up, or, maybe just sink, or float away, or I'd work up the nerve to *walk* away from it, give it up as a bum deal."

I slurp up some spaghetti. I like to eat spaghetti with a fork and a spoon, twisting it around the fork while fending off the slippery stragglers with the spoon. I look up at Robin to see how he's taking this.

"But then, Robin, little by little, like some kind of an addiction, I find myself attracted to the whole idea of living on this boat. It's been taking up an enormous part of my time and I'm way behind with my painting, but the very lunacy, difficulty, the immensity of the project, right from the beginning, has gotten into my blood. I love trying to figure out solutions to the impossible, or what seems to me impossible. Oddly enough, it's so much like painting, I suspect it was predestined. I don't have any other answer."

Barbara Austin is sitting beside me. She tosses her long hair back with a shake of her head.

"I can understand that. It must be something like having kids. It just happens to you, so your life isn't yours anymore, everything seems to blow away out of hand. Then, the more involved you become, the more bizarre it all looks. You can't back out and at the same time, you want to go on and find what comes next, how are the kids going to grow up, what'll they be like. Can I do it better than my parents did? All the questions. It's beyond your control, it just pulls you along."

"Yeah, Barb, that's a big part of it. And the same as with having kids. As you do it, you find yourself continually growing to match the challenge. I know I'm a better person in many ways for having gone through with this thing so far. I have more confidence in myself, in what I can do, but more important, I'm a hell of a lot more humble, finding out all the things I *can't* do, have no idea even how to start.

"Watching some of these river people and the kinds of problems they can handle, emergency-type situations, with such aplomb, is a revelation and amazement to me. I think it's also the feeling of being a pioneer, doing things I've never done, testing the limits of my endurance, all those sorts of experiences become important. I know when I go back to painting, I'll be a better painter because of the hellish kinds of projects I've been doing here. I'm improving my French, too. I know words for things in French now I don't even know in English. I'm learning to curse like a French sailor. *That's* mind-expanding."

I didn't intend to make such a speech, but as I'm rolling on, partly stimulated by the wine, I sense that what I'm saying is about what I'm really feeling. I stop and concentrate on the spaghetti. Rosemary has come over from where she's been pulling weeds after finishing her lasagna.

"It's really brought our family together, I can say that. Will here is never restless the way he would always be, pacing about, looking into the refrigerator, opening the door of our apartment just to look out. He seems to be more inside himself. It's almost as if this boat has become some kind of mission. I love him even more the way he is now than before.

"But it's tough for all of us. Will sweats out and dirties a full set of clothes from underpants to jeans and sweatshirts every day. His feet have begun to stink the way they used to do when we first got married. However, I'll tell you, it's nice sleeping in a bed with a hard man. His muscles are all coming back."

Neil starts laughing so wildly, I think he's going to fall off his chair.

"Rosemary, I never thought I'd hear you say you like sleeping with Will better because he has a hard muscle."

"Cut it out, Neil. You know what I mean. I'll bet Donna and Barbara know."

She's blushing. Everybody starts kidding around. Barbara and Donna laugh, too. Jo, who's been quiet all along, carefully eating, listening the way he does, looks up. He's somewhat older than the rest of us.

"Well, whatever it is, I think that boat down there is going to change your lives, and it will be for the better. I'm tempted to look around for a boat myself. I'll bet Addie would just love living on the river, and what a great studio a boat could make. I'd like to find one with a motor and learn how to drive it. I could maneuver it up and down the river and paint my eyes out. It'd make a great place to give shows from, too. Different shows in different parts of the city, different parts of France.

"Actually, with all the canals, I could paint and give shows all over Europe. Now that sounds like a great life."

We all laugh, but I think Jo has the right idea. I almost wish I still had the motor on this boat, but then I could *never* have fit the boat into this small space. I have enough on my hands anyway.

After cleaning up our picnic and bringing the chairs down into the boat again, we go back to work. The women are passing boards through the windows as we need them, and they're all helping Rosemary clean out the upper boat. It still has mud in the damnedest places you wouldn't think of, even after our big cleanup when we brought it up from the bottom.

We nail in the last boards before dark. It's like a big ballroom. Neil goes up to invite the women down to look. He's as proud as any of us at what we've done. We give them a hand down my stairway ladder. When Donna looks around, she laughs out loud.

"It's like Roseland, or one of those taxi-dance places, only on the water."

"OK, Donna, let's you and I christen this place."

Neil takes her in his arms, and they start waltzing around as he sings one of the Strauss waltzes. He has a strong baritone voice. I grab hold of Rosemary, and soon we're all dancing. Jo joins us with Barbara.

We're laughing, dancing and singing along with Neil until we're out of breath. We've combined our waltzing with something like square dancing, hooking elbows, swinging round, changing partners. Robin has started calling and clapping. I wonder what our neighbors think we're doing. It sounds like some kind of orgy. Finally we all stop and just drop to the floor. I get my breath after a few minutes. The trouble is, each time one of us starts to say something, we laugh.

"I'm promising all of you, when I have those windows in so we won't freeze, and this floor sanded down, along with some heat, and a reasonable sound system, we're going to have a celebration dance for this folly of mine."

Everybody applauds.

"Now, it's getting dark, we'd better all get home. I can't thank you enough. I never could have gotten this done by myself. Look here."

I hold up the five-kilo packet of nails; there are about ten nails left.

"We've really been pounding nails. I'm proud of us."

One by one, we climb my stairway, with me warning everyone to duck as they go up. I'll need to build some kind of wooden cushion at the top where, right now, it's sharp-cut metal just where you'd bump your head. Somebody could be scalped. As I go up, I pick out a spare scrap of Styrofoam and jam it over the sharp edge. It won't do all that much good, but for the moment it's better than nothing.

I stand and watch as each car pulls away. It's dark enough that they need their lights. I didn't really think we'd be working this late. But then, the last part we weren't working, just having an impromptu party. Matt has been good about it. I'm sure he's convinced we're all drunk. Some of those people are his teachers. I tried enticing him to dance, but he's the wrong (or the right) generation.

With a flashlight, we gather together the few nails and tools. I put them in the back of our car. Already, the paranoia of possession is creeping into things. I hate it, but as long as there are people who steal, I guess there will always be locks and people locking things up. But I'm glad for the feeling of ownership, pride in our barge, our *péniche.*

CHAPTER VIII

Smoothing Things Out

ON MONDAY, I start with the sanding. I find, in the Yellow Pages, a place not far from the boat where they rent the big industrial sanders that look like gigantic vacuum cleaners. There's no use phoning, I have a devil of a time understanding French anyway, so over a phone it's impossible.

I finally find the place. It's just a grass-grown-over dirt lot on the other side of Le Pecq. There are all sorts of equipment to rent, from shovels to bulldozers. But they do have sanders. I put down a significant deposit and buy replacement sandpaper. The guy shows me how to fit in the paper. He talks me into buying one rough emery- or Carborundum-type paper and another finer type for finishing off. He speaks simple but effective English. I'd give a lot to speak French half as well.

He also talks me into renting a long heavy-duty extension cord. I'd never have thought of it. I don't know what I'm doing trying to pretend I'm some kind of boat builder.

We manage to jam the sander into the Hillman so I don't need to put it on the roof. I don't think I could ever have lifted it back down. It's a real brute. I'm already worried about getting it through the bottom-boat window. There's no way I could pull it along that beat-up gangplank and down my ladder staircase.

I struggle it down to the water's edge. I slide the aluminum ladder in place at the window, squeeze two extra boards from the flooring job between the outside supports of the ladder and maneuver the sander onto this ramp. I push it as far as I can up this jerry-rigged ramp from the shore, half in panic that the whole thing is going to slide off right into the water or that the ladder's going to tip and off it will go.

I dash around, scramble up the old gangplank, down the steps and up onto the ramp from inside the boat. I pull, using the handle, and muscle the sander over the edge of the window into the boat. Happily, then, another gratuitous gift of the gods, the ladder tips into the boat like a seesaw and I only need to lift it off. I almost lose the two boards as the ladder bounces back onto the bank, but the gods are with me again, and the boards bounce but stay in place.

I bring down the extension cord from the car, plug it into the one heavy-duty plug I have right by the door of the wooden boat. I string out the cord down my staircase and plug it into the sander. I'm soaking wet from sweat already. I strip off my dripping shirt and hang it out over one of the riverside windows. I'm learning that in a typical day working out here, I sweat through at least three shirts. It's a bit autumnal, but I decide to work without a shirt; I'll take a shower when I go home.

When I turn on the switch of that sander, I'm practically pulled right off my feet. I've never run an industrial sander and have no idea! It pulls and bucks and I'm just barely holding on. Sawdust is flying all over the place. And when I try to turn it, about half the time, it tilts and sands a groove in the floor!

Speaking of sweat, in five minutes I'm covered with a mat of sawdust and sweat all gummed into my hairy body. And the noise. I can't hear myself think, not that I'm thinking too much. I'm too busy just trying to keep up with this devilish machine. I turn off the switch. It's suddenly deadly quiet, the ordinary quiet I'd been taking for granted. I plop down on my partly sanded floor. I stretch right out on my back and, of course, leave a big swatch of sweat. There's no way out.

I pull myself together, stand up, brace my feet and turn the switch back on. Because the sandpaper is beginning to wear down some, I have more control. I can actually begin to push the machine where I want it, instead of being dragged to wherever it wants to go.

I'm reminded of when I was about ten and I took a summer job walking an old man's dog every evening. It was a two-year-old police dog named Wolf, nice as any dog could be, which isn't very. That dog took me for walks, practically runs, all over town, to places I'd never been. Working my way back, pulling madly on the leash, to his owner's house was a major problem, sometimes taking over an hour. Well, this sander is a bit like Wolf, but not so nice.

However, that floor is getting sanded. It begins to look like a floor instead of a pile of trash lumber lined up. I'm beginning to feel somewhat in control. Then, I decide it's time I change to another roll of the heavy Carborundum paper. I lock it into place and prepare myself. I'm really surprised to find that if I just don't try to fight the thing, it isn't impossible. But it's throwing sawdust up like crazy. The hard part is getting the edges smooth around against the bulkhead of the boat without ripping off chunks of Styrofoam. But I manage.

After about two hours, I decide to try the finer sandpaper. This works beautifully, practically polishing the floor. Now I'm trying to smooth out some of the gouges I made with my first efforts, when the machine would dominate me and dig in. I've rented the machine for a half day, and it's getting to be eleven-thirty.

I unplug, roll up the extension cord, pull the ladder with the boards on it as far into the boat as I can. I hope when it seesaws on me the sander won't wind up in the river. I manage it without trouble. I'm having brief moments when I feel like a "pro" instead of a "sandpaper lotter."

I drag the beast up the bank and shove it into the back seat. I still have ten minutes. I back out down the *chemin de halage,* turn and head for the rental shop. I manage to bump down the road to the shed where the owner keeps his tools just as he's locking up. He looks at his watch, does a French shrug and helps me unload, checking to see if everything's OK, as if I could actually do anything to this machine that could possibly hurt it. I pocket my deposit and ask if he has small hand sanders as well. He nods as he's locking up again.

"Betsy there too much for you? She can be hard to handle."

"You're right there, she threw me around for a while. Sure wish you'd told me her name, maybe I could've tamed her a bit faster. Wouldn't be holding you up from *le déjeuner.*"

"'I'm open again at two, and I have some good hand sanders."

His English is really quite excellent. He sprints over to his Peugeot 104 and swings on up the dirt road. I follow him. I have a beer and a *jambon beurre* in the Hillman that I'll eat back at the boat. Now I'm beginning to have a feeling the boat is a kind of home for me, and I look forward to going back. Also, I want to puzzle out how the hell I'm going to put those windows in. I can't nail into that metal, I can't even drill holes. No glue is going to hold wood onto the edges where the windows are cut out.

Then I have an idea. I'll use the same theory I used to hold the Styrofoam on the walls.

First, after lunch, and a one-hour unplanned nap on the bank, I go back to the tool place. The guy's there and has out for me a practically brand-new-looking sander. This is a tool I've used before, but he's convinced I'm a moron now, so he shows me how to hook the sandpaper on the vibrator belt.

I make my deposit and zip on back to the boat. I want to finish sanding the stairway, braces and steps, then work around the edges and the bulkheads, where I couldn't get in with the big sander. I sand all afternoon, so my whole body begins to vibrate. Mostly I'm on my hands and knees. I find some old rags in the upstairs boat and tie them around my knees so I won't wind up with "houseboat knee."

I've rented the extension cord again so I can work the sander around to just about anywhere. But I'm beginning to lose light, so as I wrap it up I take out the last piece of sandpaper from the sander. I glance around the room and it looks great to me. I wonder what I can put on this floor to protect it, probably one of those hard-finish varnishes that comes in two cans, one with the varnish and the other with the dryer, but they cost a fortune. Also, I could just wax it or oil it; however, I'd prefer the varnish. I'll worry about that later.

The rental place closes at six and I'm running out of time. I measure all the windows and do some rough calculations. I'm hoping I won't have too much wastage from this part of the job. Money's really getting scarce.

CHAPTER IX

Money Problems

I'M BEGINNING TO go deeper and deeper into debt with all my friends. One of the advantages of being an artist is you have a chance to know a bunch of rich people. They're about the only ones who can afford a thousand dollars or more for a painting. After all, it's a mere piece of linen canvas with colored pigment ground into oil and spread over the surface, sort of expensive oil-cloth. So I've been taking advantage, hitting some of them for loans—not huge ones, never more than the cost of a painting. Most of them consider it an advance on another painting. But I'm getting deep into minus numbers, that is, salable paintings I haven't done yet.

This boat is taking all my time and money. I figure it'll take about four meters of milled, quality wood to do each window. The place I've been using doesn't carry anything like that.

After I deliver the sander back and pick up my deposit, I head out farther west. It's getting dark enough so I need headlights; the traffic is thick. I'm going to a big store called Conforama, where they sell everything, including lumber, and they're open late. I'm hoping to buy what I need with the deposit money from the sander along with a little more. I figure at the very least, I'll need fifty meters running of boards two centimeters thick and ten centimeters wide. I'm hoping I can get them in either two- or four-meter lengths. I suspect two meters for this kind of stuff is more like it. I also need some finish nails and wood putty. I'll want to make a new miter box, too, unless I can find one cheap. My old box is broken.

This place Conforama is enormous. I wander around for ten minutes just trying to find where they store the kind of wood I need. It's sort of self-serve, which is why I'm here. I have a devil of a time explaining these material complexities to a salesperson, and the French are not notorious for their patience.

Finally, I find the right area. After another ten minutes, I also find the right kind of wood for the framing, and at a reasonable price, reasonable for France. I should have enough left over to buy the quarter round I'll need to hold the glass in place.

While I'm looking, I see they're having a big sale on *frisette,* that is, wood paneling. Boy, would that boat look great with wood paneling, and it shouldn't be too hard to do if I can only figure a way to make the stuff stick to the sides of the boat. Get thee from me, Satan. I'll be in hock for more of my phantom paintings, more than the Louvre has Rembrandts.

When I pay at the cashier, I'm rooting around in the bottom of all my pockets for change. I just make it with fifty centimes left over. That's cutting it close.

I drive back to the boat, carry the loot up my gangplank and store it in the living room. I can see my work spreading out ahead of me. Except for the pleading, begging letters I'll need to write tonight, sort of like a beggar holding out his hat, it's all actually exciting and fun. I can barely wait till tomorrow.

Rosemary is great about all this boat craziness. She's worried, too, about the money, also that I'm not painting and I'm selling paintings I don't have. She knows how much I hate being in debt, but I don't really see any other way to do this. I know myself, whether it's doing a painting or working on a big project like this boat. As long as I'm enthusiastic and have the steam, I should never quit, or I might never start again. I need to keep plugging away in the flush of my excitement, while I still believe in what I'm doing.

Windows on the World

The next morning I'm out there early. First, I carry all the new wood downstairs. That gives some idea of where my head is. Already I'm thinking of this as a two-story house. I can hardly remember when it was two boats and I was out there trying to steer them one on top of the other for the great marriage. Maybe it's this kind of forgetting that keeps me going. Probably what keeps most marriages going, too.

I've brought out from Paris the bulk of my tools. I'm going to need a jigsaw, a keyhole saw, a crosscut saw, two hammers (one large, one small), the nails, putty and a miter box. I know what tools I'll be needing, but I still don't know how to put in those damnable windows. I have only a hunch.

I almost butcher the job with my first window. First, I cut the sill three centimeters longer on each side than the hole. This is on purpose. Then I jigsaw slots at a slight angle on each end of this board. I want it to slant down toward the outside of the boat to run off the rain. When all the cuts are made I fit—rather, jam—the board into place. It's tight, and I'm pleased with myself until I realize that the extra cut on each side of the window is going to make it so I can't get by with two lengths of two meter boards for each window. I'm about to pull a Ken Kesey, "take a great notion and jump in the river and drown," when I remember that the vertical cuts will be shorter by twice the width of the horizontal boards. The gods take care of drunks, children and sloppy carpenters.

I cut and fit the top piece exactly the same as the bottom so the overhang on the outside will drain the rain away from the window. Then comes the real test. I need to cut the side pieces so they'll have the right angle to compensate for the tilt outward of the top and bottom. I could measure, but I trust my eyes more than any ruler. I make the cuts and it comes out fine.

I'm so pleased I decide to reward myself by going to the café across the street, the Café Brazza, the one Alfred Sisley painted in his five paintings called *The Inundation of Port Marly*. I was so taken with the different ways he handled the sky in those paintings that I wasn't paying enough attention to the water. I should've been. Also, I'm just inside the café and am about to order when I remember I only have fifty centimes in my pocket. I smile around at the customers, the waiters, then back out. I don't even have enough to buy a box of matches and save face.

Soon, I'm thirstily back at work. I work all morning and manage five frames before my stomach tells me it's lunchtime. Thank the Lord, Rosemary packed a baguette filled with Camembert cheese with a touch of mustard, butter and mayonnaise. I fill a carafe with water, sit down on the floor of the downstairs and eat. Nothing can taste much better than a sandwich like this when a body's been working hard and is really hungry. It would be better with a nice cold beer, but beggars learn to do without.

After lunch I'm back at it. I have one frame finished while there's still light in the sky. Then I think of the miter box. I can't work tomorrow until I have one. I scrounge around, find three appropriate pieces of wood and nail them together. Using my square, I cut a straight cut, a forty-five-degree and a thirty-degree angle. I'm not about to trust my eyes, cutting angles like that on the round part of quarter round. I've learned my lesson there. I finish the job as the light is disappearing. I stash my tools in a safe place, line the wood against the bulkhead, go upstairs and then down the wobbly gangplank.

I'm a rotten backer-upper but I get out of the *chemin de halage* in the almost-dark without back-up lights. But when I roll up onto National 13, the road into Paris, the traffic is appalling. I waited just a little too long again. It takes me more than an hour to work my way through, practically playing bumper cars until I pull into our neighborhood. Then it takes another ten minutes to find a parking place. I pull my car into a mini-space for my mini-car, with only six inches to spare. It's about time we move out of Paris. God bless the English for making the Hillman with a short wheelbase.

First Things First

I dash up the sixty-six stairs and Rosemary greets me at the door with a kiss and two unopened letters in her hand. I'm still puffing, so I sit down at our big dining-room table in the middle of our living room, take a knife from the setting Rosemary's made for the meal and open them. Out of one floats a thousand-dollar check and out of the other, a check for fifteen hundred. I sure hope I get to painting again, but for now I'm dancing around the room with Rosemary and dreaming of *frisette!* We'll have the most beautiful *boiserie* this side of Versailles.

During dinner, I explain to Rosemary and the kids what I've been doing all day. I even make a little drawing so they can understand more easily. I'm really proud of my squeeze-jam system of building the window frames, putting friction on my side. Kate, our oldest, is beside me at the table. She's watching the drawing carefully. She looks up at me.

"But Dad, you're an artist. Why aren't you out there painting, instead of doing all this building of windows on a boat? Almost anybody can do that kind of work. Nobody can paint the way you do."

I lean down and kiss her.

"You're right, Kate. But I really want to have this boat fixed up so we'll have a nice place to live near school for all of us. But even better yet, I'm going to have a wonderful studio, good light and big enough for me to do anything I want. Imagine, I won't always be smearing paint over everything."

She looks at me and smiles.

"OK, then. That makes sense. But don't take too long fixing it up, or only work on it part-time. It's painting that's important."

I explain to all of them what I want the boat to be, a place that is a boat, sure, but almost like a house with big windows and individual bedrooms for everyone. We'll have a good-sized kitchen and a deck all along the river side with planters and flowers growing out of them.

"We'll even have a nice flat front deck, and most times when the weather's good, we'll eat out there. Just imagine that."

Matt, who's fifteen, leans toward me, almost spilling his soup. "And can we have a rowboat just for ourselves?"

"Sure can. We'll park it between our big boat and the shore. It'll be our own private rowboat harbor."

After dinner, I go to bed early. I'm groggy with fatigue. Maybe I'm getting into shape with all this stooping up and down, crawling around on my knees, climbing up and down that gangplank, pushing heavy things around, chasing after that monster sander, but it doesn't seem to be showing up much. I'm just tired.

One Window to the Other—I've Been Framed

I'm out there again early next morning. Rosemary, the kids and I share breakfast at seven and then scoot. She needs to beat her way all the way across Paris, just as I do, but then she needs to work her way through more traffic in the west suburb. She earns her money at that school, just with the driving, let alone teaching. She's driving our old Simca station wagon, one I bought for five hundred dollars two years ago.

I'm still driving this miracle Hillman we bought in England: Rosemary'd like to drive the Hillman, but the kids are getting too many and too big to fit. Actually, I'd be better off with the Simca because it has a large roof rack, but it doesn't work out that way.

Everything's where I left it. I start taking careful measurements on the insides of the window frames. For this, my eyes are just not enough. Cutting forty-fives on the round side of quarter round is tricky business. But it's fun. I work my way into the swing of things and in the first half hour have the outside quarter round on the first window cut and in place without too much butchery. The rest of it goes that way. On the way out to the boat, I'd stopped at our BNP bank in Garches and deposited the two checks. I have the checkbook with me.

In Le Pecq, they have another large building-supply place called Chez Mollard. It specializes in metal, kitchen and bathroom fixtures, plumbing pipes, nipples, etc. and, oddly enough, glass. I need to order the glass cut and at least three pounds of putty. I'll start out with a kilo and hope it will be enough.

I've measured each window frame carefully, watching for any differences from side to side and top to bottom. Each window is slightly different, but considering how we cut them, they're all fairly straight and square. When they aren't, I can adjust by knocking the top and bottom sills with a hammer.

I have the list of measurements with me when I drive into Chez Mollard. I drive into the very back of the yard, where they store huge sheets of glass. There's a felt-covered table for cutting. I show my measurements to the glazier there, and he asks some questions about my numbers. I always forget to put a cross through my sevens and a hat on my ones, the way the French do. I tell him I want triple-strength glass and that there are ten pieces to be cut.

I'm going to build a swinging frame for the large back window at the end of the boat. It'll swing up and hook to the ceiling so I can get furniture or large paintings in and out, but I won't buy that piece just now, I'm not sure I can fit it into the car.

He searches in his stockpile for a moment, then pulls out a large pane of glass and carefully lays it on the felt-covered table. He's marking my measurements on it with white chalk. I explain with finger and hand motions how I'd like him to cut a millimeter short on each side. I know from experience that having a piece of glass that is just a millimeter or two too large can be a short trip to madness.

He works quickly. I swear, being able to cut glass must be something one is born to. He uses the same little cutter with the rolling blade on the end that I have. He snaps that glass with the same slits on the sides of his tool that mine has, but I've never been able to manage a clean cut. He measures, marks, cuts as if it's automatic, he doesn't seem to have a consideration that it might crack or break anywhere except where he wants it to. He's careful not to waste any of his glass, picking pieces that have already been cut from the large plates stored in wooden bins behind him.

After he finishes the first one, he wraps it in newspaper on another table and hands it to me. The way he handles it, one would think it were metal or wood. I *know* it's glass, and I've broken more than one sheet of glass trying to transport it from one place to another. And this glass is heavy. I'd forgotten this about glass, but then I've never bought triple-strength glass before. This glass is more than an eighth of an inch thick. I've already decided to carry the glass in the Hillman with the back seat down. There's about five centimeters to spare sideways and ten lengthwise. I go out to back the car up close. I had no idea he'd be cutting right away. Most times when I've ordered panes of glass, I've had to wait a day or two.

Piece by piece, he cuts each plate, wraps it in newspaper, then I, nervously, carry it over to the car. I carefully slide these plates of glass in, trying not to touch the sides of the car. By pure luck, I have an old blanket that I've spread over the floor where I'm stacking. I'm glad I have my gloves with me or I'd probably cut off about half my fingers; the edges of the glass are very sharp. Using the newspapers around them helps. For one thing, I can see where the glass is when I'm trying to maneuver it into this narrow space. When it's just clear glass, it's easy to miss exactly where the edge or a corner is.

I've marked each piece he's cutting with a number on my list. And he's marking that same number on each pane of glass. We're working together with hardly a word between us. It's mostly the fact of my rotten French, but also I've found glaziers not to be big talkers. They need nerves of steel and concentration. Chatterers, such as I am, could never make it.

When he finishes, he shows how he's marked each number on the glass in the upper-right-hand corner of the plate so I'll know how to fit these irregular pieces in. I'd never have thought of it. I guess I'd have been swinging those newspaper-covered, sharp-edged glass plates around in the air trying to find the right way they fit in. There are so many ways to do things wrong.

Now he's making the calculations of the bill. I wonder if, in France, they sell glass by weight, volume or sheet. I'll never know. He hands me the bill to take up to the office. It's a maze of numbers, multiplied, divided, added.

This yard, with all its varying materials from toilets to telephone poles, with I-beams as long as fifteen meters, has *all* bills, no matter what, go through the main office up front. This is a real holdup. It takes more time for the office staff to go through volume after volume filled with plastic-covered pages, lined and counterlined, than it took the workman to cut the glass. In addition, there are long lines waiting.

Finally, a young woman takes my bill and does the calculation of how much I'm going to owe. Thank the powers that be for those magical checks, money in the pot. I hope they've cleared. I'll write my check as if they are. Then I go to another window, another line, to pay. This cashier is wearing high plastic cuffs and a green shade over his eyes, so he looks like a gambler. He examines my check carefully, looks at the bill, seemingly checking the figures, and then gives me a stamped receipt—stamped three times, that is. I don't know what to do next. The guy behind me, impatient as we all are, points to where the glass was cut, out in the yard.

I go back there, and the glazier is already cutting more glass. He takes my receipt without looking at it and spears it onto what looks like a ten-penny nail driven through a block of wood. It's almost filled to the top with other receipts.

Sliding Board with Glass

Nobody stops me as I drive carefully through the gates trying not to go over any bumps. I drive to the boat at a wicked twenty kilometers per hour and creep along the bumpy *chemin de halage*. I'm sure I'm cracking all ten panes of glass. I go by way of the *chemin de halage* because I couldn't possibly carry them to the boat from the street—they're too heavy or I'm too weak, or a combination.

But when I look in back of the car, everything seems fine. Now, how to maneuver them down the bank and into the downstairs boat. I decide to carry them one at a time. Just as well; I'd probably break my neck on the slippery muddy bank.

I have on my old work jeans so I sit down at the top of the bank and hold a glass pane over my head. Watching for branches of trees and digging my heels into the mud, I slip and slide to the bottom. This way isn't very dignified, but it's safe. I manipulate the first plate down to the water's edge. From there, I've already decided to slide the panes along the ladder with the wood liners from before. I lean out over the ladder, pushing the pane as close to the boat window hole as I can. Then, in semi-panic, tiptoeing, I clamber up the rickety gangplank, down the steep steps and reach out the window trying to catch the pane before it drops off into the drink. There's a fair amount of water movement today. I imagine some boat with a heavy load has gone by and sent wavelets up our little *bras mort* of the Seine. But, nonetheless, I do have that first pane in the bottom of the boat, safely resting on the sanded wooden floor, wrapped in slightly wrinkled and muddy newspaper.

My question now is, do I make an exploratory operation to see if I can fit this window into its waiting, wood-lined hole in the metal hull, or do I bring *all* the glass down before its too dark and before I lose my nerve. Prudence ultimately wins out.

By the time I've gotten the last sheet of glass down and into the boat, as well as being absolutely pooped, I've worn holes in each cheek of my jeans and mud has penetrated into the most amazing parts of my underpants and certain secret facets of my anatomy. I'm sure there must have been some other, better way, but it's done. I take off the destroyed jeans and wonder whether I should write to Mr. Levi and inform him of one definite weakness in his product or write a letter to Nike complimenting them on the durability of their shoes.

In the privacy of the upper boat, I do my best to scrub off some of the mud. I turn my underpants around so there is some coverage to the rear, then sneak my way back uphill to the car. I spread some old rags and newspaper over the driver's seat, and head for home. I don't exactly feel I'm retreating in defeat, but it definitely looks that way, especially from the rear.

Out Like a Light

When Rosemary and the kids see me, they howl. There's all kinds of comments about my toilet training, or who's been kicking me all over the landscape. I act up a bit, showing off the crotch of the jeans where the seam has split right to the fly. The fly is holding, but just. Finally, Rosemary stops laughing.

"I know there must be some perfectly good reason why you look like this, but I'll never figure it out. Come on, Will, let us in on the secret. I thought you were going to be installing glass in those windows. In my mind I had you neat and clean, packing in putty, sliding the windows in, tacking them lightly in place, all on this beautiful sunny day. Whatever happened to make me so wrong?"

I give them an abbreviated version of the problems with my panes of glass, my personal pains in the ass. I make a big deal out of the glazier cutting the panes from huge sheets of glass. I promise to take any one of the family who's interested to see him doing it. But I make them promise to stand quietly out of the way and not cause any fuss. I realize I should have checked before I promised. Chez Mollard probably has ten kinds of insurance reasons not to allow a band of kids wandering around the yard.

After dinner, I'm having a cup of my fake coffee called Caro when, in midsip, I catch myself falling asleep. Rosemary is across the table from me drinking her usual cup of Gentle Orange herb tea. My head dunks and I almost spill all over the table. Rosemary walks behind me.

"Come on, dear, go to bed. You're falling asleep in your cups. You've worked too hard these last few days, and it's catching up on you. Come on, now."

I don't need much coaxing. I down the last of my cooled Caro and head for the bedroom. I can hear the kids up in their play area playing Monopoly, not doing homework. The next thing I know, Rosemary is beside me, unbuttoning my shirt. I'm really out of it. She undresses me like a baby, and I'm not fighting.

"You can't go to bed like this, Will. I'll start the shower and put out your pajamas. It won't be a minute. Now don't fall asleep on me again."

The bathroom with the shower is right next to the bedroom. I hear her running the shower. I stand up, and I'm leaning on the door when she opens it.

"Will, this is too much. Come on, now, get moving, the shower will freshen you up. Be sure to wipe out all that mud between your legs and everywhere else."

For complicated reasons having to do with another of my construction projects, that is, remodeling the interior of this old carpenter shop into an apartment, the shower is up two steps to provide drainage. Rosemary stands there with the soap in her hands until I'm inside, and she pulls the curtains.

She pushes soap through to me. The water is just right. That's one of the advantages of being married to the same woman for a long time—she knows exactly how hot and how hard I like my shower. I know she doesn't like hers as hard or as hot as I do. Our special knowledge comes from years of trying to take showers together.

I slowly start scrubbing myself in the crotch. Boy, I am really stuffed with black, gooey mud. The water in the bottom of the shower begins to look like the Mississippi, dark and muddy. Rosemary's hand reaches in again, a palm filled with shampoo.

"I know you don't have much hair, Will, but what you have is all caked with mud. And don't forget to wash the back of your neck."

I wash my hair and let the soapy water run down my body. I lean against the shower wall in front of me and just let the water coat me with a fine film. It's like a gentle massage.

We couldn't fit a tub into this tiny bathroom, so it's this elevated shower. I've fallen asleep often in tubs in my long life, but this is the first time I find myself falling asleep in the shower. I start sliding slowly into the Mississippi.

Luckily, Rosemary looks in at the precise moment I'm ready to let it all go and try curling up in the bottom of the shower.

It couldn't be too bad; we've given the kids plenty of baths in the bottom of this shower.

But she rouses me, dries me off, as I halfheartedly, half-assedly, try to help. At least, so she tells me much later. I don't remember anything after I've scrubbed the shampoo into my dirty, thinning hair. She must also have worked me into my pajamas, because when I wake in the morning, I'm wearing them.

Tricky Business

Rosemary and the whole crew are gone. There's a note on the table beside my plate where she's set my breakfast.

Hope you're feeling better, Will. Please don't go to work on the boat today. You need a rest. I have a faculty meeting this afternoon so we'll be late coming home.

Love you, Rosemary.

I pour out Muesli cereal and spoon yogurt onto it. I drink my orange juice, washing down the vitamins she's left on the place mat. I chop a banana into the cereal, stir up the mix and eat it. I'm not tired anymore; in fact, I feel as if I've just been born again. I can hardly wait to be out there on the boat pushing glass into place. I'll make a point of getting home before five. Rosemary won't be home before then, what with the faculty meeting, so she won't have time to worry.

I look at my watch for the first time. Nine o'clock. I haven't slept this late in years, not since before we had our first baby, Kate. I scoop out the last of the cereal, wash it down with the orange juice that's left, take the dishes into the kitchen, and wash them. The dishes from the family's breakfast are in the dish rack, dry. I add mine to theirs. Then I go into the bedroom, make the bed and dress myself in another pair of work jeans.

The traffic isn't too bad, and I'm climbing up the gangplank before my wristwatch beeps ten.

The sun's out, but it's cool inside the hull of the boat. I keep on my jacket as I work. I cut a set of the quarter round for the inside of the window to the same measurements as the exterior ones. I open one of my packets of putty, work and roll it around in my hands to warm and soften it, then, using a spatula, start squeezing putty in all around the first, outside, set of quarter round that is in place. I slip on my gloves before lifting the pane of glass, then I stack the tiny glazier points in place on the sill under the window.

I feel whole and intact, doing quiet, constructive work on a cool, sunny morning, floating on a river. Slanted beams of sunlight splash on my newly laid and sanded wooden floor. I'm at one with the world.

Happily, because I'd put the panes of glass into the car in the order in which they'd been cut, when I unloaded them, they're reversed and in perfect order where I stacked them in the boat, with the number-one pane on top. I check my gloves once more and take a deep breath.

I put the number-one in the upper-right-hand corner, and it slides in perfectly. I push the pane in against the putty just tightly enough to hold and, hopefully, keep out the rain. Some extra putty slides visible between quarter round and glass but, after all, this is only the first pane. Nothing's perfect.

Now, holding one hand up against the glass, just in case the putty isn't strong enough to hold it in place, I pick up the piece of quarter round I'd cut for the top inside and spread putty along it, but not too thickly. The glass fits into place beautifully. I'm holding the window in now by leaning against it. I hang some of the tiny, headless points between my lips and position one in the center of the quarter round. In my back pocket I have the little tacking hammer I usually use to nail canvas onto stretchers. I use it now to hammer in the small point. I'm getting nervous. I hammer along the same plane as the pane of glass, tenderly, cautiously. It goes in easily. Now I feel safer.

Over the next quarter-hour, I position all four quarter-round pieces in place with putty, and nail three of the small points in each. The fits at the corners aren't always exactly right, but I didn't really expect them to be, only hoped. I'm on the last nail, the right vertical quarter round, the hardest one, because I can't nail left-handed. I'm twisted around to nail properly parallel to the plane of the pane when I do it. I mishit and the point nips the pane so a small crack spreads out of the corner!

At first, I think of throwing the hammer through the window, but control myself. I rub a smidgen of putty along the crack line and wipe it off. I also wipe off all the window because it's smudged with putty. When I'm finished, I stand back to take a look. Not perfect, but good for me. I swear I can already feel the boat getting warmer.

I work all day putting in windows. That first crack is the only one. After that, I hammer with the caution of a kitten fishing goldfish from a bowl.

I stretch out on the floor and look around. It's definitely warmer now. I'm going to need to build that back window so it can open, not only to move large things such as paintings into or out of the studio, but for ventilation.

I've never built a real window before. I measure around carefully for the big window. Tomorrow I'll go buy materials. I've actually spent the entire day doing just what Rosemary thought I'd be doing yesterday. It was demanding work but not butt-busting. I'm clean, except my undershirt is soaked with nervous sweat. I forgot to eat lunch, but then I had a late breakfast.

It's just before four, so I hide my tools, sweep up bits and pieces. I'd like to go search out materials for making that back window, but I can never do that and be home by five. As I go up the stairs, I look back, and it's beautiful. I swear, because of the white Styrofoam on the walls and the light coming through the windows, it's even lighter than outside; what a great studio it's going to be down there. I'll need water and a way to drain it without sinking the boat, but that comes later; the draining, not sinking the boat, I hope. Tomorrow it's the back window.

I'm not quite home by five, but I luck out on a parking place and beat the rest of the family into the apartment. I pick up the mail and the *International Herald Tribune* at our mailbox in the entry hall. I'm aching to take a shower before they come home, change into a sweat suit, and be lounging around like a rock star when they come in, but I'm too tired. I only change my shirt. I've just settled down in my favorite chair when I hear them on the stairs. Rosemary unlocks the door. She stares at me and smiles.

"Well, you really did it. I never believed you'd actually take off a day from that dumb boat. What did you have to eat?"

"I had a great breakfast, even ate a banana for the potassium."

"Well, how are you feeling? You look fine."

She puts her wrist against my head.

"Here I left a virtual corpse in the morning and come back to find you lolling around good as new. That's wonderful."

The kids go change out of their school clothes. Rosemary carries groceries into the kitchen.

"How about a cup of Caro, dear? I'm having some tea. Those faculty meetings can be so dumb. We don't talk about the children, or the curriculum, or anything that matters, it's only about money, the budget, salaries and *'Formation Professional.'* One English teacher wants money to study pottery on a Greek island. Maybe she's going to teach her students how to write cuneiform on clay tablets. I don't know. Maybe I'm in the wrong profession."

The Back Window

Next day, I look all over for a place where I can buy materials to build my back window. It turns out to be a small wood and molding shop up in St.-Germain-en-Laye, about three kilometers from the houseboat. Most of the other places I'd been to would make the window for me but wouldn't sell the raw materials so I could do it myself.

This place has a nice woman who agrees to help. The shop is very tiny and in a narrow back alley not too far from the post office. I show my measurements to her and she searches through her stock until she finds something I can use. I want the most simple materials possible. I'm not even considering building a window with individual panes. I want to look out that opening with nothing between me and the view but clear glass.

She says she'll sell me the glass and extras I hadn't thought of for constructing the window. I know the glass will cost more here than at Chez Mollard, but this is a straight cash deal, no standing around in lines before people with celluloid cuffs. I generally prefer dealing with small artisans. These people are just holding on by their teeth in France, particularly specialty businesses where they custom-build windows, furniture, metal work for balcony railings and so forth.

After a morning of futile running around, it looks as if I'll finally have the materials to build our window. The woman gives me several hints as to how I should go about it. She also sells me hinges, special wood glue, some more putty, a pair of latches to keep the window shut and a screen-door hook and eye to latch the window to the ceiling when I open it all the way, if I ever manage to have a real ceiling. She speaks slow, simple French, so she almost makes me believe I understand the language. She tells me her husband is out putting in a whole set of twenty windows in an old office building. He custom-built them all, right here in this little shop.

I've built enough stretchers and frames for paintings, so I'm not too worried about this job. To be honest, I look forward to it. I'm tired of all the brute labor. Even putting those raw panes of glass in my hokey frames was a bit too much like heavy labor for me, especially when I think about sliding down the bank, then running back and forth from the riverbank, up the old gangplank, down the stairs, then leaning out the window and pulling those heavy panes in.

I watch her cut my piece of glass. It's twice the size of the others, and I'm as amazed as I was at Mollard's when she snaps off the huge piece clean. I try to help her, but she waves me away. I guess it's a one-man (woman) job. I'd screw it up for sure. When I heft this pane into the back of my Hillman, I'm even more impressed. It's heavy and that lady can't be more than five feet tall and weighs less than a hundred pounds. She says it's all in knowing how to handle the glass. Ha!

She helps me cushion the pane so it won't break on the trip back. This time the pane barely fits on the blanket; it's twice as long as the other panes. I'd measured before I left, to be sure, but until it's actually in the car and the hatch closed, I worry. I'm a worrier. I wave goodbye and she goes back into the little shop, wiping her hands on a blue denim apron and smiling.

I use the same system I used before to haul the glass down to the boat: more mud up my rear end. However, this glass is so long it wants to bend, and glass won't bend. I'm sure it's going to crack in half and I'll be cut at least in half. But by going slowly and not jiggling too much, I make it. Less mud, too—most of it is in the plumbing at our apartment. I have a regular mudslide down the *berge* now, curved to fit my contours. I'm slipping in the mud, like an otter except I don't go all the way down into the water, on purpose.

Sliding the glass onto the ladder and wooden trestle is, of course, even more of a project, but I do wrestle that large pane into the boat and settle it on the floor. I sit beside it, dripping sweat.

Building the frame, as I thought, turns out not to be too big a deal. I keep squaring it with my square as I go along. Fitting it into the frame so I can attach it to the boat, as I did with the smaller windows, is another problem. This time I really need to measure carefully so the frame will fit the frame of the window, no half-baked measures now. I put quarter round only on the inside. This means I'll need to do everything inside out, from under the window.

The window will open in, hinged to the ceiling as I planned it. I don't have any wood on the ceiling to which I can attach the window when it's open. This additional luxury will need to wait until I've lined the inside of the boat with *frisette*. . . . If!

But it doesn't matter. I'll latch it closed for now, and when I want it open I'll jam a piece of wood against the frame to allow air to come in. But I'm getting too far ahead of myself, always dangerous.

However, I'm learning something. I suspect the frame with the glass in it is going to be too heavy for me to mount without help. Still, I'm anxious to get along with the job. I decide to hang the window frame first, then put the glass in *after* it's hinged into place.

First, I check to see if the pane of glass fits in the window frame. It does. I lift the glass out and put it well aside so I can't step on it.

Then I start the process of fitting the window frame into the mounted frame on the back wall of the boat and attaching it with the hinges. After this, I mount the attachments the lady sold me to hold the frame shut. This seemingly simple operation takes me two hours. I spend another half hour opening and closing, latching the empty window frame, congratulating myself.

My hands are shaking and I realize I've forgotten lunch. I go across to the café and have a *jambon beurre*, the ham sandwich with butter on half a loaf of French bread. I spread mustard on the ham in the sandwich and wash it down with a *demi*, a small glass of French beer. The sun is shining and my hands have stopped shaking. It just wouldn't do to try manipulating that glass with shaking hands. I talk to the woman who runs the café. She's been watching the progress of the boat, too, each time she takes her dog for a walk along the *chemin de halage*. She says she's impressed, at least that's how I translate her rapid-fire French.

I go back to the boat. I'm sure it'll be a tough afternoon, but I'm feeling as ready as I'll ever be. Naturally, the glass must be fitted into the *outside* of the window frame. This means I need to crawl under the frame I've just mounted on hinges at the top and squeeze myself along with the monster piece of glass *between* the window frame and the back wall. I'm working up a panic again.

I squeeze myself into place, then realize I don't have my hammer, the little glazier points or the putty to hold the glass. I can see them on the floor through the glass too far away for me to reach. So I need to reverse the entire procedure, lower myself— with the pane of glass—out from under the window frame, then slide the glass to the floor without cutting off my toes. I require another rest after these contortions.

Now I balance my hammer, the glazier points and putty on the sill.

I don't own a putty knife, so I do my damnedest to work in the putty with a kitchen knife. It takes forever, although this must be the two-hundredth window I've puttied in during my life as amateur builder. When it looks fairly good, not too much putty showing from the inside of the windowpane, I wipe off all the smears, putty, sweat, exhalations, until *voilà*! There's a window with a regular God-given painting framed for me looking upriver to paint, if I ever find time to paint again.

CHAPTER X

Time Passes and Then the Gangplank

DURING THE NEXT days, weeks, months, years, every time I manage to squirrel enough money to buy a few packets of *frisette,* I'm down in the hull of the boat nailing it up. I don't think I could have faced doing it all at once, so this is one time our economic shortcomings are to my advantage. As I'm working on the walls, framing with paneling and molding the frames of the windows, I keep looking up at the ceiling, that is, at the Styrofoam that is still jammed in the places where I hope to put a wood ceiling. The great difficulty will be getting around the line of metal supports we left from front to back of the boat. They stick down about half a foot, with sharp triangular-shaped braces on each side every half meter. At the lowest point, they're only about six-and-a-half feet from the floor.

I come up with two solutions. I'll try the first one in the room where the stairs come down from upstairs. It'll give a sort of W-like configuration. Since my names, first and last, start with Ws, it's appropriate.

In the meantime I continue with my slow wall-paneling and actually build a halfway-mark divider and hang two interior doors. They're made from two pieces of light plywood, framed on the interior with cross-bracing wood. They're wide enough to move most furniture or any large paintings through them. I build two, one on each side of the center line, where we've left a section of wall for additional support of the deck holding the upstairs boat.

I'm finding this part fun and, in addition, I'm actually back to painting, real painting, my own paintings.

My main effort now is to renovate the upstairs, then the gang-plank, so the family can move out here and live. Then there will be no more hour-long trips through Paris in the mornings. Also, I can start staying at the boat. I never thought that would sound so good.

I find old rugs on the island across from us. It's an outfit like the Salvation Army called *Les Frères Emmaus* or, sometimes, *Abbé Pierre's*. It's named after the priest who founded it. They clean out attics and cellars, and people give them stuff they don't have any use for, but is too good to throw away. Every time I drive out the N13 road to the boat, I stop and look, hoping to find something they have that will be OK on the boat.

Rugs are the first things I buy. They're in various tones of tan or beige. It makes the place look lighter and more civilized. The rugs I put into my original upstairs pirate's-den version were ruined in the inundation.

I also find a table and some chairs, simple but strong, well glued. I'm not exactly fighting the antique dealers who show up in all their finery looking for that lost Louis XV armoire. I even replace most of our pots and pans, cutlery, dishes, so the place is ready to move into. These pots and pans are ten times better than what we have at home in the apartment. Our apartment is pretty much furnished with used junk anyway. I mean, most of it was already used when we picked it up years ago. Then, after fifteen years of use by a family of five, it's well *used*.

Next, I work on the gangplank. It's too short to be of much use with the door of the wooden boat way up on the upper edge of the metal boat. The old gangplank won't do at all, except as a sort of ladder. If I'm going to have Rosemary and the kids live out here, it's got to be better than that.

I go back to the lumberyard where I bought the roof-beam boards for my steps. This time I'm really getting into something. I calculate that, with the boat pulled as close to the shore as I can manage, cranking away daily with my winches, I'll need boards at least six meters long to make a gangplank that won't resemble some kind of obstacle course. Even so, I'll also need a system to lift the land end if the water rises.

It's the same man in the yard. He remembers me. We go again into the special shed for these long beams. I actually find two beams eight meters long, that's almost twenty-seven feet. We slide them out and line them up next to the car. Then I line myself up at the office. It turns out, I could actually buy a first-class stereo system for the cost of those two beams, but there's no other way if we're going to live on the boat; we can't cross the water on the music of Mozart or Bach. I can't ask the family to climb in through the windows.

I shouldn't even go into how I struggle those boards to the boat, but I will. Obviously, they'll absolutely smash in the car roof. Also, they're more than twice as long as the car.

After I've paid and tried dragging one of the boards myself along the *chemin de halage* to the boat, making about five meters, getting nowhere, I ask Matt to give me a hand. His friend Tom and another friend of their's, Sam, agree to help. Sam has only one arm. He lost his other arm making rocket fuel which exploded, for a handmade rocket more than three years before we bought the boat. He was only about thirteen when it happened.

I drive them out on Saturday. They're all impressed with how the downstairs boat is coming along. I show them how I hope to hook the gangplank to the bollards on each side of the doorway to the upper boat, and then have a system for lifting the shore end.

Sam, who's lived on houseboats with his parents most of his life, has good ideas and stops me from making at least ten different serious errors. I'm impressed. It's difficult to accept all the ways a boat can frustrate the best intentions a certified landlubber such as I might have.

At the lumberyard, we each put a rope sling over our shoulders and under the boards. At first we try two boards at a time, but that obviously won't work. However, we can make it by hauling one board with the four of us carrying. Of course, this makes two trips. At the instigation of Matt, we go along the *chemin de halage* singing "Yo ho heave ho."

When we have the two boards at the bank, the problem is to lift the heavy ends up to and over the edge of the upper boat. Sam comes up with the best way. He scampers one-armedly up the old gangplank. We throw our rope slings up to him. He ties them together to make one long rope, then, along with Matt up there, Tom and me at the bottom, using the bollard of the upper boat to brace against, they pull the ends of the beams up over the edge. It's a sweaty job, but finally both beams are in place spanning the water and up two-thirds of the bank. We tie them to those old bollards of the upper boat on each side of the door, using one-handed knots Sam knows how to tie. By drilling a hole at the end of each beam for the rope to go through, we fasten them tightly to the bollards.

I'm ready to quit, but this band of bandits wants to go buy short boards to nail onto these big beams so we'll actually have a gangplank. Sam slides, standing up, arm waving, down one of the boards like a tightrope walker. If he does that kind of thing all the time, I figure he's lucky to have lost only one arm. He's going to break his neck. I didn't know Sam yet. He has no more fear of heights or danger than a panther.

We measure to Sam's exacting standards (he thinks in millimeters) and head back to the lumberyard. We hope to catch them before noon, when they close. We buy the same kind of wood I'd used to cover the floor of the lower boat, only we buy shorter pieces because they're cheaper. I'm using up the cash I'd put away for my *frisette* faster than I can think. But now we're really moving along. When we get back, Sam and Matt have it all planned out. Tom and I are put to cutting planks to make the gangplank. They're leaving about a quarter inch between planks. Sam insists we drive in only one large nail in each plank because with the crappy (his term) mooring system I have, this boat is going to budge back and forth about three or four feet at a time when the Seine starts pitching and rolling. These boards need to be able to swing with the movement or they'll split, according to Sam.

It's OK with me. I don't exactly relish the idea of hammering on that slanting gangplank anyway. And, quickly, it's becoming a *gang*plank all right. Soon, all four of us are up there; it happens before our eyes. Two hammering, two cutting boards. In just that afternoon, we have it done. I can't believe it.

Sam shows me how I can use the outside heavy beams from the old gangplank to erect verticals on either side of our new gangplank with braces underneath and between. This would enable us to lift the end of the gangplank as the boat rises with the water. He wants this contraption just about at water's edge. He says it will also keep the gangplank from shifting too much with the ebb and flow of the river. All I need do is drill big holes in those old boards, set them in cement, then buy an iron bar at Chez Mollard to pass under the gangplank and through the holes. The idea is that I move up the iron bar into the higher holes as the water rises. It all seems like overkill to me, but then I don't yet know the force and unpredictability of this river. That will come soon enough.

Sam, with that left hand of his, makes good drawings of what I need to do. He's holding the paper with his stump and drawing like a draftsman. I'm amazed. With this drawing, even I can build this "Bridge Over the River Quay." As darkness falls, we drive home.

Chapter XI

Family Arrangements

In the morning, Sunday, that is, I invite the rest of the family to see how our boat is coming along. They are properly impressed. If they weren't, I'd have divorced the whole kit and caboodle of them. The gangplank is a great success. I show off some of the furniture and rugs I've been buying. Rosemary likes the things I chose.

Now we start figuring out where everyone is going to sleep. At first, Matt wants to sleep in the crew cabin, but to go down in there, he'd need to come out from the house part of the boat, walk across the deck and climb down the ladder through the hatch. Matt doesn't especially look forward to that, particularly with winter coming on.

One of the things I found at *Abbé Pierre's* is a three-quarter bed with a good mattress and drawers for storage under it. The wood is oak and the handles on the drawers are brass. I don't know how it wound up there at *Abbé Pierre's* but it's perfect for our boat. The question is whether Rosemary and I will sleep on that bed in the living room, in front of the first large-view window. If so, the girls would sleep in the back bedroom. An alternative is that we sleep back there, with the girls in this new bed and Matt roughing it out in the crew cabin. There's also a small entry into which we could put a tiny bed, big enough for Camille. She's the youngest and the shortest. The bed can't be more than five feet long, but it tucks nicely into a corner there above where the steps go down into the lower boat.

We figure we'll work it out. In fact, we do right there. We decide Kate will sleep on the bed in the living room, the new one. Rosemary and I will be in the back bedroom, and Camille will sleep in the entry. Matt will be sleeping in the crew cabin; he's gone up and down the steps several times out there now and is comfortable with the idea. I promise I'll bring light and heat down into the room. He'll have space to store all his clothes, his airplanes, chemicals, animal and plant collections. Generally, storage is going to be a serious problem on the boat.

Matt tries out the bed. It was definitely built for a small French sailor, but by sleeping corner to corner, it's big enough. Matt stretches out on it and is excited with the whole idea.

Only Kate is anxious about the boat sinking. I don't blame her, but I've become convinced that with this metal hull, we're safe. Every time some methane gas explodes, like a whale fart from under the boat, she jumps. Also, sleeping in that bed, she'd be sleeping right over where the board blew out when the upper boat sank. I try not making too much of that. I wasn't going to tell her at all, but figured it wouldn't be quite fair. But then, the wooden boat isn't even in the water now, so it doesn't matter.

Downstairs, I show how I can divide that whole space into a writing room and office for Rosemary and me, a painting studio, and a small apartment in the area behind the steps. Matt or Camille can sleep back there when I have that part finished. Rosemary will have another small office in our bedroom with a desk along the right side as she comes in.

We make a list of the things I need to buy, especially the small bed for Camille, bed sheets, covers, all of which we'll buy at *Abbé Pierre*'s. They dry-clean everything that comes in, so it isn't exactly a true flea market. We take a walk along the *chemin de halage* and look into some of the other boats. Most of them are fascinating, with lovely plantings and ingenious gangplanks. Even though it's a bit cold, there are men playing on the *boule* court.

We drive home with everybody excited. It seems that, after all, we'll actually be living on the boat and soon I can have a studio out here with place to paint and places to store paintings. One of the miseries of being a painter is that one doesn't sell them all. This is inconvenient in terms of survival, but even more inconvenient, because they soon begin to take up a big part of one's living space.

Back to Painting

I'll build painting-storage racks in the center section downstairs two tiers high, with the same system I used in my Paris studio before it burnt down, that is, tough nylon strings woven up and down from ceiling to floor, held by big staples. First I'll need to build a framework to pound the staples into, but that shouldn't take long. Considering everything that's gone on so far and what still needs to be done, it's nothing, and it will certainly improve my life.

I'll tell you, being surrounded by hundreds of paintings while you're trying to concentrate on one—the one on the easel in front of you, the one that's going to be the best painting you've ever made—can seem futile sometimes. But that's part of what being a professional painter is all about. A good painter somehow always remains an amateur at heart, a lover, a lover of his work.

Monday, *Abbé Pierre's* is closed and I don't have any spare cash anyway, so I bring out my paintbox and a painting easel. Driving to the boat, I tie the easel on the roof of the poor Hillman. That roof is beginning to look a little the worse for wear.

Then, I set the easel up by that back window in the lower boat and paint the first of what will become a large number of river paintings. The pirate boat with its forecastle and upper deck is beautiful on the right side of the painting. My Breton neighbor sees me and smiles. That's the first smile from her.

I paint away all morning, working up the drawing and under-painting. I discover how important sap green and raw sienna are in the painting of river water, at least Seine River water. I also dis-cover the river is getting more green than the black it was when I first saw this boat. Also the smell is definitely improved, or else I'm immune now.

It's a sunny day. I have a lunch packed and sit at our new table, new to us, anyway. The chairs are comfortable as well as strong. I feel I've moved in. All I need is one of those captain's caps with the little bill on front, the kind M. Teurnier always wears. It's probably as good as a beret for hiding my bald pate.

I not only have the water functioning, but also the water heater, so now I can wash my few dishes. The boat is beginning to seem a friendly place, not just a locale for mortal combat. I decide to clean things up, sweeping all the upstairs, mopping and wiping anyplace where there's still mud we didn't find before. I'll need to put *frisette* over the lower parts of the walls. The water has ruined the brocade I'd put on before. The brocade on the ceiling seems all right. I'll go along with some of the paste I have left from when I put it up in the first place, stick it back up again where it's hanging down. I pull off the brocade on the walls I'll need to replace.

Temporarily, I'll nail over this part with simple imitation wood paneling that comes like plywood. It has grain and grooves to make it look more real. It'll be enough for now. If I do any more actual wood paneling after I finish the bottom boat, I'll probably turn into some kind of tongue-in-groove man.

Chapter XII

Moving In!

I MAKE UP the beds with the new sheets and the blankets from *Abbé Pierre*. The place is beginning to look homey all right. I wipe off and wash everything in the kitchen. Actually, the women had already done this while we were laying the wood floor downstairs. I think I'm just going around putting my personal mark on things. I can be like that. I imagine it's an archetypal form of marking possession, like dogs or wolves.

I rig a railing to hold on to when coming up the gangplank. I keep looking around for things that should be done before we start living out here. We have heat, the catalytic butane heaters and two electric heaters with oil inside them. Electricity heats the oil, so they radiate.

As I said, we have water. The john is working, even though one needs to go up two steps to sit on it like a throne. I've rigged a PCV pipe from the toilet outlet on the upper boat to run down the outside of the lower boat and into the water. I need to find a septic tank small enough to fit into the back of the lower boat and still large enough for our family. That will come.

I should put in for a phone. I don't think this will take too long. The Frenchman from whom I bought this boat had a phone put in and paid for poles all along the *berge* for the phone line. I'll call from the apartment for somebody to come out and install it.

I buy some Styrofoam at the building-supply place, two-centimeter-thick sheets, and spread them on the floor of the upper boat. I cover the Styrofoam with carpets, my *Abbé Pierre* carpets. After I have them spread around, it feels like walking on deep pile rugs. So, as far as I'm concerned, once more we're ready to live on a houseboat.

That weekend we move in. Friends help by lending us three American-style station wagons, and we bring everything of any value from the apartment out on the boat in two trips.

Our lease on the apartment is up at the end of the month, so that's no problem. Now we'll do a mad clean-up job to bring that apartment into the kind of pristine condition the French expect after they rent to someone. They actually expect it to look better than it did when the renter moved in. This one sure as hell does. But we're accustomed to this. Next weekend, that will be the project.

I'll work all the week on the apartment first, doing the heavy work like shampooing carpets and cleaning the woodwork, then we'll just scrub and paint. Our kids will help out. We've moved often enough.

The entire family seems content with the idea of living on a boat. I hang used inner tubes all around the sides. I buy them for almost nothing from a big place in Paris where they sell new tires. I paint them white with black stripes. These are mostly patched and not very impressive, but I have ropes tied tight to them, so if anyone falls in, we can throw one of these out and pull the victim in.

That Saturday night, we sit around, almost forgetting we're actually floating on the water. There's virtually no movement, and with the drapes from the apartment, hung up and pulled closed, we're independent of the world. I begin to wish there were some way I could pull up that gangplank, like a drawbridge for a medieval castle, so we'd really be cut off.

Sunday morning, the sun comes out and shines through the windows on the river side of the boat. We have breakfast in that sunlight, croissants from the baker just up the street. We're all bubbling over, like playing house.

Monday, they all go off to school. Camille looks back as she goes down the gangplank with her schoolbag over her shoulder.

"Gee, Dad, it's like a real house. Nobody at school will believe me."

Tying Things Up

The next days and weeks I try to divide between working on the boat and painting. I need paintings to pay off my debts. The family seems to enjoy living on the boat, especially not having to make the long trip in from Paris.

In a month I've finished eight paintings, river paintings. I've painted looking both ways from the roof of the upper boat. The roof is made of metal with ridge lines running horizontally. It's great being up there—I have views up and down the Seine, from where it curves going up to Paris to where it curves around the island.

I also paint from the docking stage of the boat club, about two hundred meters from our boat, away from Paris. Monet, Sisley and Renoir painted from here a hundred years or so ago. This gives me a different perspective, down low, because the dock from which they launch the sculls is at water level. It's great because there aren't too many people hanging around, the way it is when I paint in the Paris streets.

Meanwhile, I divide my time between tacking up *frisette* in the lower boat and shoveling away at the sandbar so I can tuck the back end of the boat in where it belongs. I finally do get it almost lined up with the other boats. I find lengths of cable on the *berge* all coiled up under some abandoned wood. I pull it out and spread it along the *chemin de halage*. I'm wearing heavy gloves because the cable has needlelike barbs from where some of the outside strands of the cable have rusted and broken. When I have it spread out, I can see that although it doesn't look so great, it's strong, and I can use it to tie the boat to the bank.

But before that, I check with both my neighbors to see if this cable belongs to either of them. Begrudgingly, they tell me it belonged to the man who owned the boat before me. I figure, finders-keepers.

At Chez Mollard, I buy a six-foot-long solid steel bar about two inches thick. I'll drive this into the top of the bank with a sledgehammer I found in the bottom of the metal boat, covered with oil. The handle of the sledge was rotted, but I bought a new handle at the hardware store in Le Pecq. It must be a ten-pounder and gives me a great feeling of power.

I dig a hole about two feet deep and fill it with concrete. Then I drive the steel bar into the wet concrete and through into the dirt below. I swing that sledge and watch with joyful wonder as the bar sinks in about half an inch with each of my swings. I drive it down until only about a foot and a half sticks up out of the concrete. I've tilted the bar at an angle away from the boat to keep the cable from slipping off. I stamp down on the concrete around the bar.

I tie my cable to the back bollard of the metal boat with a pair of half hitches, then hook a rope to the other end of the cable and tie a rock to the end of the rope. After about three tries, I manage to heave that rock up onto the bank. I rush around to retrieve it before the weight of the cable and rock pull it back into the water.

Now I need my winch again. I keep it tied to the same tree I was using to pull the boat in from the sandbar. I run it up and around the newly sunken steel bar. I have the cable locked through the hook of the winch. I start cranking until the cable is tight around the bar, the boat pulling in perhaps another six inches. Then, I pull on the end of the cable, make a tie around the bar and finish with a pair of half hitches in opposite directions so it's almost like a square knot.

When I loosen the winch, the cable stays taut and the bar is firmly sunk in the cement without budging. I go through the same procedure at the front of the boat. I figure that should hold. I don't know, now, how I could have been so naive.

Skiing and Swimming Al Fresco

Winter comes, and the American school has a ski trip up into the Alps at a place just across the French border in an Italian ski resort called Bardonecchia. Rosemary and I are asked to chaperone and help with the sponsors of the trip in exchange for free transportation, free hotels with meals, even free ski passes for all the family. We can't resist; the kids are as excited as we are, or even more. We sign up. The trip is in February.

Already, in January, the river has been rising. I keep tightening my cables and adjusting the *perches. Perches* are long poles attached to the boat and tied to trees on the bank to keep the boat away from the land. The big cables pull the boat toward the land, the *perches* keep it from floating up onto the land and perhaps getting stranded there. I feel I'm finally becoming something of a river man. I continue adjusting the height of the gangplank, moving the iron bar up another pair of holes in the support, according to the plan Sam has devised. I keep ahead of the rising water easily. I'm not too worried. Things seem to be working as planned.

Our ski trip is everything we had hoped for. No one in the family is hurt, and the kids all improve their skiing. Rosemary and I ski our usual snowplow-cautious ways down the easiest slopes but have a good time. We are returned by bus to the school, where we have our car parked. Then, we drive from school with our considerable luggage to a bizarre sight!

First of all, when we come around the corner at the café, our boat and all the other boats along the *berge* look as if they've been lifted out of the water to be on exhibition. Shocked, confused, we dash forward. The river has risen and is more than a meter deep *over* the *chemin de halage* itself! The river is five meters up, over fifteen feet higher than normal! Our boat is swung out at an angle again, almost perpendicular to the *berge,* and the gangplank is holding on to the boat, but the land end of the gangplank has swung with the current at a cockeyed angle!

I can't even think of any way to board if we wanted to. Our neighbors are running around like crazy people, fastening things down and cursing us for abandoning our boat!! The beautiful black or green Seine is a raging, yellow muddy river now; it looks like the Amazon, with rippling waves as the water courses along its rampaging way. The river has risen so completely, it's covered the island across from us so it looks like one huge wild river with whitecaps all the way to the bank on the other side of the island.

We drop our bags, and I strip down to my skiing long johns. I wade into the cold, roaring river up to my chest and make an attempt to pull the gangplank back into place. The current is unbelievably strong; it almost sweeps me away. Matt strips and comes in to help. With much struggling, we manage to fasten the wayward gangplank with a piece of rope to a tree upriver. This we do with a rope I'd left in the high crotch of a tree after one of my last transports on the roof of the Hillman. Thank God it's still there, barely above the water.

We find out that the town, in the emergency, is supplying what look like heavy sawhorses to anyone who needs them. Not only has the river flooded its banks, but it's all the way up into the streets in most parts of town. We manage to commandeer two of the heavy sawhorses and tie them to the upstream tree. We also tie them to the gangplank, which we lift with great difficulty onto these sawhorses. The gangplank is bucking and surging, trying to break away. I crawl out on it, not looking down into the wild river. From the front deck, I unhook the heavy metal ladder we first used to go down into and out of the metal hull when we were clearing out the oil.

I drag it down to where the bottom of our gangplank disappears into the surging water on the *chemin de halage*. Matt jams the other end into the bank leading up to the slightly above-water *boule* courts across from us. We tie this, too, to another upriver tree. Next, I scramble back onto the deck and carry some leftover planks from the downstairs flooring and fit them over the metal ladder. Now, we almost have a functioning gangplank we can use to board the boat.

Rosemary and the girls, with the luggage, have retreated to the café. The café is just barely out of the water. Men are piling sandbags in front of it. Mr. Sisley would have loved all this, but not me! Matt and I go back to grab our bags before they are washed away. It's the first time I notice the crowds watching me in my long johns and Matt in his Skivvies hustling around madly in the freezing cold.

Like drunken acrobats, we carry the luggage across the gangplank and store them inside the boat. It's so strange, with all the action and noise outside, the boat seems calm, floating above it all. But it's very damp and cold. I check to see if the electricity is still working, and it is. I start the electric heaters and light the butane heaters: Considering our dress, Matt and I should feel colder than we do. Wonderful stuff, adrenaline.

The question now is, does the family spend the night on the boat with me, or do we hunt up a hotel where they can stay overnight.

After we have the last of the luggage stowed on board, I scurry down our newly wobbly, makeshift gangplank, then wade through the water again. I want to see if that iron bar I'd driven in so deeply on the bank is secure. It's OK, but the support system with which

I was supposed to lift the gangplank is completely underwater! I can even see it, but definitely can't reach it.

I run to the back of the boat and find that the knot I tied in the cable to the bollard has slipped, and that's been the trouble. I scramble and splash through the water to rescue our winch. Matt and I hook the cable to the winch, pull taut, then wrap the cable around the bollard. We start cranking, pulling the boat back in toward shore. Whatever sandbar might once have been is long gone. The current is incredible, sending splashes up at us on the upper boat. When we have the boat hauled back in, we fasten it tightly.

Rosemary and the girls come down to look at the situation. Matt and I maneuver our aluminum ladder, the one I bought to build my stairway from upper to lower boat, and tie it down to the gangplank along with the other ladder. We anchor it to the fence surrounding the *boule* court, which is about a foot above water. The angle of the gangplank up to the boat is frightening.

Matt, using the sledge, drives stakes on the downriver side of the ladder, and we tie the whole mess together. We put more planks on the top ladder. We also string a rope tightly from the boat, at the door all the way to the *boule*-court fence. If anybody's going to walk this plank, they'll need something to hold on to. Even pirates might be a bit squeamish.

Rosemary decides we all ought to stay. I'll move our car up higher into town so it won't be inundated. We'll commandeer some more sawhorses and planks from the town. It seems we've done all we can for now, and both Matt and I are starting to shiver, although the boat is warming up.

The first thing after we're all settled in, Matt and I take showers. We check if there's anything to eat. It's Sunday night and no stores are open, but there are some eggs, butter, a can of string beans and a package of noodles. There's also a well-aged baguette we bought for the train on the way home. We find some wine and apple juice.

So we have a nice meal, feeling like frontier people fighting the elements. Matt and I have put on sweat suits and rescued out clothes from where we stripped them off; the river is still creeping up. It's well over the *boule* court now.

Matt decides to sleep up on the floor of the living room instead of down in the crew cabin. He says the roar of the water against the side of the boat down there would keep anyone awake.

We gather together all the flashlights and candles we can muster, so everybody has some kind of light if the electricity goes off. I climb in bed knowing that early tomorrow I'll need to climb up on the roof of the upper boat with a Swedish bow saw and cut off some of the branches that normally hang romantically over the boat. They're now trying to press their way through the roof and *into* the boat. That's about all we'd need, leaks in the roof. The last thing I do is set my wrist alarm to go off every two hours. I go zoom deeply to sleep. I didn't sleep much in the *couchette* coming from Italy.

CHAPTER XIII

Digging Out

IT TAKES A lot longer for the water to go down than it took to go up. I paint a calibrated line on one of the trees beside the gangplank and mark it every day.

At first, the river keeps right at its high-water mark, and there isn't much change for almost four days. I ask around concerning where all the water can be coming from because it isn't raining at all in Port Marly or in Paris. The skies are blue and high with a few racing clouds and bright sun.

I find out that it's been raining all over France, and just about every river is overflowing. It seems the wonderful snow on which we skied in Bardonecchia was part of the same precipitation that is causing the flooding. The good news is that *La Navigation* has declared the flood tide has been reached and we can expect the water to go down, unless there are more storms up the Marne, the Eure, or the Yonne.

I go back, check my marks, and nothing's changed. I wonder what would happen if it started teeming rain right here on the Seine, then realize that most of it would be downriver from us and wouldn't matter.

The next day, sure enough, the river starts to go down, over two inches that day. When I look out the next morning, it's down a good foot. At breakfast, we celebrate with croissants instead of our usual bread and butter. I'm wondering what I can do to avoid the same kind of catastrophe with other rains and floods.

Everything is covered with mud up to where the water has risen. I buy a plastic hose at Le Couier, the hardware store in Le Pecq. I buy two lengths to make fifty meters of hose. I figure with this, I can reach all parts of the boat and gangplank that are coated with the mud. It reminds me of squirting mud off all the furniture as I pulled it from the wooden boat the first time. Am I going to spend the rest of my life spraying mud off everything we own?

I can now take the aluminum ladder off the bottom of the gangplank. I see the surface of the *chemin de halage* about three feet down. The heavy metal ladder with the boards on it will be enough for the family to climb up onto the gangplank. As the water goes down, of course, the steepness of the gangplank decreases. I decide when this mess is cleaned up somewhat, I'm going to nail one-inch strips of wood along the gangplank so it will be easier to climb up and down without slipping.

I search out my bow saw, actually my Swedish imitation of same, lean the ladder from the gangplank against the roof of the boat and climb up into the foliage of the trees hanging over the roof. I inspect and no serious damage has been done. I start by cutting off the branches that are actually gouging the roof. I throw the branches I cut off the roof into the still raging Seine. They're biodegradable. There's a regular flotilla of branches floating past the boat all day long. The flood's ripped out just about any vegetation that could be uprooted.

I cut away all morning and, after about two hours, have quite a pile of willow branches on the roof. I trim any branch that comes within a meter or so of the boat. That should give me another meter or more of flooding without any damage. If it goes any higher than that, I'll have more to worry about than just the roof.

When I come off the roof, the water's receded another half foot. I squirt with the hose, the trees, the gangplank, anything I can see with mud clinging to it. I notice M. Le Clerc, my down-river neighbor, doing the same thing. We wave to each other. Maybe finally I'll be accepted into this hermitlike boating community. Bad enough that I don't know the first thing about boats, but I'm an American. How low can one sink? I know how low, just as low as this boat could sink and then ram into *his* boat. I definitely need to discover some better way of mooring our boat.

Sam to the Rescue

I'm squirting away, beginning to think of lunch, when Sam, our hero, casually walks up the gangplank as if it's the aisle of a church. I turn off the water. Sam is checking the cables that have stretched considerably in the rush of the flood. He's wearing rubber boots.

"Hey, Sam, want to buy a boat, slightly used but very cheap?"

"Hi. Matt's been telling me about what's been going on out here, so I took off from school today to see just what's happening. Our boat's fine, rode right up with the water, didn't even need to adjust a cable."

"Well, as you can see, the water's gone down almost a meter here, and I've been spending my time washing off the mud from everything and trimming the trees so they won't drive their way through the roof."

Sam points behind me.

"What happened to your *perches*?"

I looked where I'd braced them rather lightly. They're gone and I hadn't even noticed.

"Guess they got washed away in all the confusion."

"I was afraid of that. You'll need to work out a complete new system for mooring this boat or the whole thing's going to wash downriver with the next flood. I think I have an idea of what we can do to keep *La Navigation* happy and I don't think it will cost too much. They'll never let you get by with tying to a tree after this flood, especially after they've put in all that work keeping your boat in place. They'll probably be sending you a bill. You know there were pictures in two French newspapers of this boat about ready to take off for Rouen. You'll be hearing from the head of *Navigation* in the next few days."

That's all I need. I look at the mess the boat is in now. My pride and joy is only a mass of twisted cables and mud, with a gangplank skewed all out of joint. I'm about ready to give up again, but not Sam. He's inspecting the cables and ropes holding the boat in place temporarily. He does his dance up the gangplank.

"It won't take much to fix this so they won't have a thing to complain about. It'll cost some money, but when we're done, you can come through a flood as high as seven meters without having to adjust even one cable. It'll all go up like an elevator in a sixteenth-arrondissement apartment."

I look at my unhappy boat. I realize the reason the gangplank has twisted so is that it was bearing all the weight of the water pushing against the boat trying to shoot the whole shebang up on the *chemin de halage,* or maybe even up on the *boule* court, or, as Sam says, on a Normandy beach. Now that would really be trouble. I look at Sam. He's back climbing around inspecting what Matt and I did.

"OK, Sam, how much? I'm just about running totally short on liquid money. Liquid river I've got, but money is something else."

He shimmies up the gangplank, using a tree to brace himself. He doesn't even wet his boots.

"Let's go inside and I'll explain how we can do it."

In the boat, I hunt up a pencil and some paper. He spreads this out on our table. He hunches over it with his arm wrapped around the top of the paper the way you'd expect a lefty to write, even a lefty by default. He has his head down close to the paper. He explains as he draws along. He doesn't use a ruler or guide of any kind. He has such control, he can make a straight line or a curve totally freehandedly.

"You see, the problem is to have your cables and *perches* attached to the boat and the land at exactly the same level so they're parallel to each other." He draws this in quickly. "Also, we should have cross-cabling to stop the boat from shifting up- and downriver with every ripple in the water the way its been doing. Then we can drive two more nails into each of the boards on that gangplank because we won't need to worry about the boards splitting. It'll be a lot stronger then."

He looks up to see if I'm with him. I nod. He's making it all very clear, maybe too clear.

"I really think the first thing you should do is replace that rusting cable. It's not going to hold anything if there's a *serious* flood."

He's drawing away. If this wasn't a serious flood, I hate to think what one would be. This was just about as bad as Mr. Sisley's flood, at least from what I can see in the paintings—and they were done almost a hundred years ago. I watch to see what he's doing next. He's drawing inverted cubes up where the cables would be tied.

"Now, this is the hard part, and I can't see any way around it. We need to dig holes here and here."

He points with his pencil.

"These holes need to be deep enough to hold two to three yards of concrete at least one meter deep. Into each of these, we drive two I-beams two meters long. They need to be at least fourteen-centimeter beams. But if we do this, and are tied tight to them, your boat will never budge. You won't have a worry left in the world."

How do I tell him I won't have a *cent* left either and I'm too old to dig two holes that deep and mix that much concrete? Those days are gone forever. Maybe if I were twenty, yes, perhaps even thirty. But now? No way. He goes on. It's as if he's reading my mind.

"I have a friend just up the road in Louveciennes who has an old backhoe. He mostly does ditch digging for people putting in sewers or things like that. But he never uses it at night, so it just sits there. I'm sure we can borrow it from him, and it won't cost much at all. I know how to use one and it's so close by we won't have any hauling or transportation costs."

My God, he's serious! How did I ever get into all this, and how can I get out of it? Should I?

"With that backhoe, I can dig those two holes in three hours, clean as a whistle. My dad has a spotlight we can borrow, and you'll just stand on the bank and hold it so I can see what I'm doing. It'll be great fun. I love using big machines like that. Maybe we can find some other places we can dig things up, too."

He's raring to go. He uses the phone on the boat to call this friend with the backhoe. Backhoe doesn't actually mean much to me, except a hoe one must use backward. I don't see how he can dig these holes he's talking about, using *any* kind of machine, especially with only one arm to run it.

But we're on. He babbles away in French on the phone. When he puts the phone down he's smiling. I'm hoping the smile means the guy just laughed in his face, but no. For only two hundred francs, we can have the backhoe any night after seven, till midnight. Sam is jubilant.

Concrete Evidence

"We'll wait till that water goes down another meter, then we'll start. The ground should be soft and be no problem at all. I'm sure the last of the water will be off the *chemin de halage* by then. First, we can buy our concrete at the big sand and gravel place in

Sartrouville. That way, we can skip the middleman and have the concrete mixed while they're rolling from there to the boat."

I'm listening, in fact I'm all ears and antennae. How can I stop all this without hurting Sam's feelings and, I'm wondering if they'll take my new *Carte Bleu* to pay for all this. I've had it only a month and haven't used it yet. There's no money in the bank, so until we can get some, it doesn't mean anything anyway. I wonder how the French law takes care of a case like this. Is it fraud?

But I don't seem able to come up with anything to stop all this from happening. I'm paralyzed. The size of the project, the way we would be doing it, my total inexperience, and worst of all, my penury and unwillingness to admit to it, all gang up on me while I'm listening to Sam.

He says the water should be back down enough by the end of the week. He'll check with Tom and Matt to see if they can help, especially with the concrete. He wants me to drive him to Sartrouville right now so we can put in our order. I don't under-stand why we don't just telephone, but when we arrive there, I know why.

It's only about a fifteen-minute drive. We turn into a terrible conglomerate of large dump trucks, small pickup trucks and enor-mous concrete-mixing trucks. We park in an unused corner of this mêlée and stride across the wet yellow combination of sand, earth and gravel that covers everything at the base of a huge tower. Under the legs of the tower is a cement truck, and great metal slides are pouring in quantities of sand, gravel and cement. The noise is deafening. Added to it is the sound of both sand and gravel being moved up to the top by bucketed moving belts.

Sam asks a few questions and motions me to follow him. We start up a stairway around the outside of this seething tower, on metal steps at an angle steeper than my gangplank at the worst moment of flood. Sam is dashing up those two steps at a time. The steps are perforated metal so I can see through to the concrete-mixing truck and all the activity below. I'm about ready to close my eyes, sit down, turn around and inch my way back to the ground. Sam looks back at me and waits.

"Come on, you'll get used to it. It only *looks* high. We aren't much higher up than a ten-story building. It isn't much farther, come on."

He's started his loping again, two steps at a time. I look back and see some workmen coming up behind us. I'm trapped. Even I, with my massive cowardice, could never inch my way, on my duff, past these heavy-footed men with their yellow construction hats.

I close my eyes, grab hold tight to the thin metal pipe inside railing and continue, inching a step at a time as those behind me shake the entire structure with their heavy thumping feet. After what seems two years, I open my eyes, and there's Sam leaning over the railing on the outside, looking to see if I'm still behind him. I close my eyes and brace myself for the inevitable tumbling crash to the yellow mud below. When I open them again, I'm only about ten feet from a platform where Sam is waiting. I count those last steps and smile sheepishly. Sam is gentleman enough not to say anything. I'm already worrying about getting back down!

Sam knocks on the door of a small cabin at the top of this miniature Leaning Tower of Pisa. We go in. It smells thickly of tobacco smoke, old sweat, obscenities and concrete. My vocabulary of French obscenity is becoming greater than my entire scope of the French language.

Sam uses his stump to work his way to a desk in the corner. Nobody seems to be objecting to his pushing up to the front. Maybe I've discovered one advantage to having only one arm.

Later, I ask Sam about it and he says that wasn't it, it's just that most of these men work for big construction companies and come up here to laugh and chat with the guys. This is something they enjoy; they're in no hurry. They're mostly drivers of the concrete trucks, which is no fun in itself. When they're on the work site, they need to regulate the flow of concrete into the hampers, a filthy, dangerous and fatiguing job.

Sam apparently gets our order in and arranges for delivery at the boat the coming Saturday. He uses my credit card and then folds the receipt into his pocket. I begin to understand why nobody minds Sam's butting into line. They're as afraid as I am of going down that metal matchstick of a staircase.

We go out and I stay just one step behind Sam all the way, keeping my eyes focused on his back. I'm halfway down before I can risk a look over the side, and it's worse than I'd imagined. I'm stopped cold, and it takes almost a minute to make myself begin walking down again. Sam waits for me but doesn't say anything. He must think I'm a real wimp. I guess I am. I'm not particularly afraid of heights, not as bad as Matt or Rosemary, but this is just too much of a test for me.

We get back to the boat, and Sam starts right away dragging boards from everywhere on the boat and piling them on the gangplank. He searches out my two hammers and the nails I have left. I'm just watching him; he smiles up at me as he lines the boards on the outside edge of the still-descending gangplank.

"I'll bet tomorrow we can start building those forms in the holes for the concrete."

He says this while the *chemin de halage* is still under almost a foot of water. But I have to admit it is going down fast now. I've got to face it sooner or later. Up till now I've been afraid to ask.

"Sam, what can I pay you for all this work? Do you work by the hour or the day, or what? I could never get these things done alone."

He smiles his sweet, reasonable smile again and shakes his head.

"No way. I love doing projects like this. The only trouble is I can't keep skipping school all the time. Pollicott, the Vice Principal, will have my ass. Maybe we'll put off building the forms another day. I only have one class in the afternoons on Fridays. I'll be here by ten, and we can get to work."

"But you can't just work like this for nothing. You have special skills and knowledge. I have to pay for your time at least."

"OK, let's say a hundred francs a day. But you don't need to pay except when you have the money."

"That's a good deal for me. I'll have some money by Saturday, and I'll pay you then. I need a rest, too, to finish up some paintings I've started."

That night, I tell Rosemary about climbing up the monster tower to buy the concrete. She says l should let Sam do crazy things like that if he wants to, but I should know better. I tell her how we've decided I'll pay him a hundred francs a day when he's working on the boat.

"How about Tom and Matt? They're working, too."

I hadn't thought of that. I can't be paying out three hundred francs a day or we'll be broke in a hurry. I'll need to think about it.

That evening and all the next day, I work to finish up three paintings I'd already gotten up to different points between drawing and final glazing. They come out great, considering the little time I have, and the pressure. I end up Thursday night making simple baguette frames for new ones.

CHAPTER XIV

Two Holes in One

FRIDAY, WHEN I drive up to the boat, Sam's already there. He's pulling the wood off the gangplank and piling it up on the *chemin de halage* near where we'll be doing the digging. He says he's skipped his second-period class and taken the RER train out. He has the sledgehammer and has sharpened some of the two-by-four-sized boards so we can drive them in at the corners where we want the hole. The water has gone down considerably; it's about half a foot lower than the level of the *chemin de halage*.

We work all day driving in those posts, cutting and nailing the boards to them. We aren't going all the way down into the hole with our form, just deep enough to stop the concrete from flowing away over the edge of the hole. I can't believe how Sam has it worked out and how hard he works. He'd be worth more than a hundred francs a day if he didn't do anything at all, just figured things out. But, in reality, he works three times as fast and as hard as I do. He always seems to know just what's the next thing that needs to be done, then how to do it. The more I work with him, the more I wonder what it is I've been learning all my life.

We have the forms built and dirt packed on the outside of them as it starts to turn dark. Dirt, hell, I should say mud. It's like clay not quite ready for turning into pots. Sam shows me the light he's borrowed from his dad and the extension cord that we'll run along the gangplank and into the heavy-duty socket I used for running the sander. When we switch this on, it's really bright. Sam shows me where I'm to stand for each part of the work as we dig. He's telephoned his friend with the backhoe again, and things are all set for six o'clock.

Just then, the rest of the family comes home. They're astonished at what we've done, just as I am. Sam is anxious to be off and pick up the backhoe, but Rosemary talks him into staying on with us for dinner. Sam calls home so they know where he is. Rosemary goes to the phone and talks to Barbara, Sam's mother, and tries to explain what's going on and how he's invited to dinner with us. Sam comes back on the phone and says he won't be late and she shouldn't worry. I've wondered if there was someone worrying about Sam, besides me.

We sort of rush through dinner—spaghetti with meatballs and fruit cocktail for dessert. I eat faster than I should most of the time, but Sam, with his one hand, just shovels it in. He cuts the spaghetti with his fork, then sort of slides it to the edge of the plate and pushes it into his mouth. At a quarter to six, we're on our way.

We arrive at Sam's friend's house in plenty of time, and Sam drives the backhoe in front of my car along route N13. I keep on my emergency flashers just behind him because he can't go any faster than twenty kilometers an hour. It's peak traffic, and we're sitting ducks, easy targets for some of these wild French drivers dashing home for dinner. Luckily, their aim isn't too good; so we make it to the boat.

Not only have I never seen a backhoe, I've never really watched one in operation. I've driven by street repairs going on but never actually taken the time to look. Sam rolls in beside the *boule* court and onto the *chemin de halage*. He lines the backhoe up with our hole, and after I've switched on the light, starts dropping the hoe down into the hole and scraping away. It's a tough balancing act as he carefully lowers the mouth of the hoe inside the forms and scrapes away. It reminds me a bit of the oil wells along the road in Los Angeles. It's like a big bird taking drinks out of a dish.

When he pulls the hoe out filled with dirt, he lifts it high and swings over with the machine to the downhill side of the hole, dumping the load into the water. He explains over the noise of the machine how we're lucky we don't need to rent a truck and carry the dirt off. I can't help but worry about the Le Clercs when all this mud rolls up against their boat. But then, the water is so muddy anyway, they probably won't notice.

Sam keeps digging away, somehow avoiding the forms we've put in and pulling the dirt out carefully. It's somewhat like watching a swallow build a nest with mud. Every so often, he has me take a rule and drop it into the hole to see how deep it is. He has calculated we'll need to go down at least a meter or we'll have concrete left over. Right there is an idea that could give me nightmares.

As soon as the first hole is finished, he whirls the backhoe and rolls along the *chemin de halage* to the place for the other hole. It all goes as before, except some of the dirt is beginning to pile up on the fence between the Le Clercs' and our place. Sam insists it will all wash away or if not, when the water is down some more, I can take a stiff broom along with my hose and brush it away. He's been right about things so far, so I just take it on faith.

We finish the second hole at about eleven o'clock. He's promised to have the backhoe returned to the owner by midnight. Matt's been out helping us, holding the light sometimes, or measuring. There's nothing much more we can do, except when one of the forms begins to float up a bit, we give it a few whacks with the sledge. Matt's as impressed as I am. It is amazing to watch Sam run this machine, almost as if it's some kind of toy.

The last thing, after we're finished, we hose off the backhoe, washing away all the mud before we return it. When we're finished, it looks clean enough from what we can see with the lamp. Matt lights Sam's way back to the road from the *chemin de halage* while I go up and turn my car around.

We ease our way out onto N13 again. The traffic isn't so bad at this time of night, but I keep cringing, expecting one of these madmen speeders to just run up my back. But all goes well.

When we finally make it, I give the two hundred francs to Sam, who, in turn, gives it to the owner of the backhoe, who, after checking over his machine, takes it, and I presume, goes to bed. Then I drive Sam up to the RER and he catches one of the last trains back to Paris. I drive home to the boat and am more than glad to snuggle into bed with Rosemary. It's been a long day.

On Saturday, Sam and Tom arrive at about nine-thirty. The concrete truck is supposed to arrive at ten. I'm standing on the gangplank, squirting mud off things as they rise clear of the water. I also see the enormous yellow concrete truck breaking and cutting its way through M. Le Clerc's beautiful willow trees. There go the beginnings of my somewhat tenuous friendship with my downriver neighbor. These trees of his hang out over the path, and there's just no way to slide this twelve-foot-high monster past without a little impromptu trimming. I just hope all the noise won't wake the Le Clerc family. Some kind of suit, *procès,* the French call it, would be what I don't need at this point. But *c'est la vie.*

The three of us start working madly to build a splashboard and slide for the concrete when it swooshes down from the truck into the hole. We don't have time to build two, so we'll shift it to the second hole after we've poured the first.

Sam posts us all where he wants us when the pouring starts. We watch as the truck, like an enormous sea monster working its way through seaweed, emerges. Sam indicates where he wants the concrete poured. He speaks good, American-accented French. The driver hops down from the cab and looks. He nods. He swings the slide for the concrete around and lines it up with our hole. Sam puts another brace on our splashboard. Matt and I are on either side of the hole with shovels. Tom is bracing the slide trough brace with his feet. We're ready—at least as ready as we'll ever be. The mixer has been turning all the time. The man at the control for the concrete slide shouts to the driver of the truck, who's leaning out the door to see what's going on. Sam gives the signal and the concrete starts pouring out, solid-state oatmeal mush, splashing all over us. It's going well, and I'm beginning to swallow the lump in my throat. I've never liked oatmeal anyway.

Matt and I are pushing the concrete from the center out toward the sides of the hole. It's sure coming out fast! Sam's watching the level carefully. He's the first to see that the forms are beginning to float, to lift. He springs through the air, over the concrete, like an antelope, and balances himself on the post that is lifting. He signals the operator to hold the concrete. Sam has us level off the concrete already poured. He turns to Tom.

"Tom, go find the sledge. I think it's just inside the door where I put it last night. Hurry!"

Tom lets go of the brace for the splashboard, dashes across the *chemin de halage,* pulls himself up onto the gangplank and runs to the door. Rosemary is standing there holding the sledge out for him. I notice the rest of the family is standing there at the door watching this (so far) near debacle. Tom comes running back with the sledgehammer. Sam is still balancing himself on the post.

"Tom, I'm going to shift my weight from the post to the two boards nailed to each side of it. When I do that, you give a few hard whacks on top of the post where I've been standing. I think that should be enough."

Tom nods. Sam jumps to the edges of the planks, and Tom starts pounding on the post. It goes down about four more inches. Sam stays on the side boards. He gives the signal to the guy operating the concrete slide to start the concrete again. He makes a sign with his hand and says, in French, *"Lentement."* Slowly.

Like an orchestra conductor, Sam directs the concrete pouring until it's up to the tops of the forms. He signals for a stop, and Matt and I continue shoveling the concrete and making a smooth top surface. Tom has found two huge rocks somewhere and puts them one on each side of the post so Sam can get down. Sam lowers himself slowly, and it all stays in place. We find another board and lay it across the forms, over the concrete, and load it with all the stones and rocks we can find. The truck has moved to the other hole. We carefully take off our concrete slide board and start installing it there. So far, so good, but I'm dripping with nervous sweat and some honest sweat. Sam is cool as a Popsicle. Tom and Matt have worked up a sweat, too.

The pouring of the second hole is about like the first, except the forms don't float. I'm amazed again when we use up exactly the amount of concrete left and the hole is just filled when we're finished. Tom, Sam and Matt put another board across the top of the poured concrete, resting on the forms as before, topping it with rocks, while I help the drivers clean off the concrete on their truck with our hose. I keep looking back at what we've just finished and can't believe it. It's only about five minutes to eleven. We've managed to have all that concrete poured in less than an hour. The concrete truck drives off, more impromptu trimming of the willows. I look, but nobody seems to be watching from the Le Clerc boat. I'll try to straighten it all out later.

When the truck's driven off, Sam checks everything and gathers us together.

"Now we've got to hustle over to Chez Mollard and buy the I-beams to pound in before the concrete sets. I'd meant to do it yesterday, but there wasn't time. I have my heavy drill, and we'll need to drill holes in each of the I-beams, so we won't have much time. I called Mollard this morning, and they close for lunch at noon, so we'd better be on our way. These babies are going to be heavy. Drilling and pounding them in isn't going to be any picnic either."

So we gather up rope, a blanket and some planks that Sam insists upon to put on the roof of the car so the weight will be distributed. We're off for Mollard's by eleven-thirty. It seems as if we're always rushing. I imagine when one is working with concrete it's like that. Time, tide and concrete wait for no man.

We're there twenty minutes before they close. Sam directs us back to the section where I'd bought my steel bars and my first I-beam. Nobody looks particularly happy to see us. But Sam knows exactly what we want and points them out. I go into the first office to make arrangements and then to the front office to pay before they close *me* out. Rosemary was paid, so I have some money now. I give Sam his two hundred francs and Tom, with some reluctance, takes another hundred. Matt won't take any.

"Come on, Dad, it's my boat, too, you know."

I don't argue too hard. I'm pleased he feels this way. I love the idea of family, of family helping each other, of everybody being part of what's going on.

When I come back, they've already loaded four huge I-beams on the roof. Even with Sam's planks to distribute the weight, the roof's sagging. After I give the man in the yard my receipt from the office and while everybody is hanging around to see us out, Sam motions me over to another part of the yard. It's where they store great rolls of chain, all sizes. He walks over to one of the biggest, with links a quarter of an inch thick and each link more than an inch long.

"That's what you need to hold your boat in place. It's galvanized and will never rust. After all this work, it'd be dumb tying the boat up with that rusty, rotting cable you have there."

I nod. I'm beginning to be afraid these guys here at Mollard are about to throw us out. One thing you don't do is delay a Frenchman from his lunch; *laissez-faire* and all, but first things first. I'm also a bit concerned they might come chasing us for another reason. I paid for the I-beams with my *Carte Bleu* again. It was so much faster that way, and everybody was in a hurry. I'll put some money into the BNP with a check tonight.

We pile into the car. We're absolutely riding on the shocks. How much shock can a shock absorber absorb? Do they go into shock? I ease us out of there into the lunchtime traffic. Sam suggests we don't try driving down the *chemin de halage* because we might get stuck in the mud, and besides, it's too bumpy, so we park up on the road. We carefully slide one of the I-beams from the top of the car, scraping as little paint off the top as we can. Poor Hillman. It's called a Hillman Husky, but it isn't *that* husky!

It takes all four of us to carry each of those beams down to the *chemin de halage*. I can't imagine how they managed to heft them up onto the roof. Maybe the guy in the yard at Mollard's helped them, probably just to rush us out of there.

When we have the four beams down on the *chemin de halage,* I'm ready for lunch. I figure we'll all go across to Sisley's café and have ham or cheese sandwiches with some beer. But I didn't figure on Sam and concrete.

"Hey, you guys, first we've got to push these babies into that concrete before it begins to set. And when we do it, we'll need to make sure we don't start the forms floating again. We should be drilling those holes in the beams, too, but we'll need to do that when they're in place; now, it'll probably be better because then we can line up the holes. So, we'll keep these stones and planks in place. We can stand on the plank to give us some leverage when we start pounding with the sledge."

Sam climbs up onto the plank, placing his feet near the edge of the form, especially on the downhill side, where the pressure is the greatest. Tom, Matt and I puff and strain until we've got one beam up to Sam and vertical. He lines it up near the middle of the block, then lifts and plunges it in, wiggling it back and forth as it settles down.

Tom then climbs up and starts pounding on top of the beam.

He pounds until he can't lift the sledge anymore. Then Matt climbs up and takes his swings. By the time it's my turn, the I-beam is almost as deep as we want it. Sam has set it straight up and down, not tilted the way mine was. I ask about this and he tells me he'll explain later, but it will be all right. We're in his hands. I wonder if Matt and Tom are as confused as I am.

Now we take the next beam and do our best to work it vertical and as close to the other beam as Sam wants it. He's twisting it so the beams are exactly parallel. Then he begins to rock this beam back and forth until it's obviously through the concrete. Again, we start pounding it in, till it's the same depth as the first one. Sam has been running around with another, smaller sledge smacking this beam to keep it parallel. We're all about ready to drop.

I stagger over to the second concrete "deadman" behind Sam, along with Tom and Matt. I'm finding out how the age difference really cuts one down. I'm hoping there will be some difficulties to slow us up so I can recoup my strength. But no. Sam is standing up on the edge of the deadman, motioning Matt and Tom to push one of the two remaining I-beams up to him and vertical. I give a shove with all my strength to help clear the edge of the form. Sam goes through the same actions as with the last one, working it into place and level.

"Now, Tom, knock it down in and I'll stand over here at the post so there's no chance the form will float up."

He sets himself into position, and Tom picks up the sledge-hammer and starts to swing. He takes ten healthy cuts, then puts down the head of the sledge so Matt can continue. Sam is measuring all along. Matt tries to match Tom, but Sam calls him off after eight swings. Sam jumps down and measures the height of the beam sticking above the concrete. He lowers his eye and sights on the first concrete deadman and the posts over there. He seems satisfied.

"OK, now we'll set in this last beam and we can go fill up our stomachs."

He checks to see if the form is floating. It's fine. He climbs up again. Tom, Matt and I struggle with the last beam. We have just enough strength to fix it in the right spot of drying concrete so Sam can maneuver it into position. He wiggles it a few times using his whole body, holding it against his chest with his left arm and right stump. He's still balancing on those boards around the concrete. He gives the sign that we should start with the pounding.

It's my turn, so I climb up on the opposite corner and start swinging with all my might. Twice I miss and just barely avoid hitting Sam on his booted foot. I manage seven swings and then I'm totally kaput. Tom takes over and, with his ninth swing, pounds it in deep enough to satisfy Sam. Sam packs the concrete around the two beams after he's sure they're level enough. He jumps down and wipes his hand, covered with concrete, on his jeans.

"Well, that's something worth having done, I'd say. Where can we find something to eat around here?"

I give up on my idea of feeding them at the café. I look at my watch. It's twelve-thirty. The *routier* restaurant down the street should be open. They give a good, hearty meal for fifty francs, and no sandwich at a café is going to be enough for these three, or me, after this morning's work. I tell them what I have in mind. By the smiles all around, I know I'm right. We're about ready to leave when Rosemary comes out onto the gangplank.

"Come on in. You guys must be starved. I've cooked a chicken and made a pizza. We also have some beer."

There are even bigger smiles on their faces. This is better than any *restaurant de routier* could give us. We start washing the cement off our hands, faces, boots. We leave the boots on the gangplank. Even so, we're a fairly raunchy bunch when we sit down. We wipe out that chicken and pizza, even destroying a big bowl of salad.

CHAPTER XV

Dead Man Tales

AFTER LUNCH, WE sit down while Sam draws out his idea for connecting the big *perches* to hold the boat in place, that is, away from the land in high flood. It turns out, he explains, that Mollard doesn't carry a long-enough length of metal tubing to reach from the deadmen, with their I-beams, to the bollards of the metal boat, where he intends to attach them. He's investigated in a catalog and found two different lengths that would fit together like parts of a telescope.

He'll then, after we have them in place, drill a hole through to keep them from sliding. It sounds look a good idea. I hate to think of the cost for such a system, but after all the concrete and beams, not counting the entire cost of the boat, it's the only solution, Sam explains.

"We can go now to pick them up. But first, this is how we'll do the hookup.

"On the quay it will be easy. I'll drill big holes through the two beams in line, then we'll drill holes in the *perches* so we can slide a pin through the beams and through the *perche* on the inside of the beams. They can swing up and down with any flooding or rocking of the boat, and still have enough give for sideways motion when necessary, but not too much."

He draws this out so we all have the idea. I have to admit it's a great solution. I nod along with the others. I feel for my card in my pocket. "In for a penny, in for a pound," or maybe that should be "in for a centime, in for a franc"—lots of francs, phantom francs, like my phantom paintings. More likely, in for a couple years, at the least—in prison, that is. It'll give me time to write more letters to my painting constituents. I won't tell them how I'm spending the money, or where I am; they'd never believe me anyway.

Sam continues drawing. This time it's more complex.

"On the boat, at each of the bollards we'll make a collar out of strip metal. We'll wrap it around the bollard under the ties and drill holes through the ends. We'll also drill holes through the *perches* so we can do the same kind of connection we've done on the land. It should work fine, and I'm sure we can get everything we need at Mollard's."

Great, I think, but what are we doing with *perches* anyway? I've had many birds in my life and I've always made perches for them, that I understand. In fact, a part of my dream for this boat is to have an aviary on the back end of the boat, but *perches,* now? I'm also somewhat concerned about going back to Mollard's after using my empty new card this morning and now using it this afternoon. I still haven't had a chance to deposit money in the account; things have just been going too fast. I don't tell the boys anything about my worries—no sense ruining their lives.

Telescopic Perches

So, we go to Chez Mollard again, around a corner to where they store their longest bars and tubes of metal. Sam finds what he's looking for, and the four of us pull out the pieces he indicates. They're heavy! I take the bill up to the office again. When I come back, all relieved, with *PAYÉ* stamped on it, they've already tied two of the poles to the roof of the car. Each is eight meters long—

that's about twenty-five feet! Sam walks around the car, jumps on the back bumper.

"I think Tom and I should stay here while you take these to the boat. The two of you can unload them on the *chemin de halage* if you lift off one end at a time."

We agree to this, so we leave Tom and Sam in the yard while we cautiously work our way back through Le Pecq. We have a real struggle unloading these metal tubes, even with Sam's parting instructions.

When we drive back into Mollard's, they've already been experimenting with sliding one tube into the other. Sam's torn between sliding the one all the way into the other or carrying them separately the way we did the first two. I can't believe it.

"Wait a minute, Sam. Matt and I could just barely lift a single one off the roof of the car. We're in no real hurry."

"OK, then we'll take them apart again and tie them on the same way as before."

"Sam, you're an absolute madman. We'll all wind up with double hernias."

It's a little bit like the chicken, the fox and the grain as to whether we should carry these two to the boat, leaving two of us here in the yard, or try to make it with all four of us *plus* the two metal tubes. We decide to risk it.

And we make it. A couple times I'm ready to give in but don't say anything. Sam suggests that all three of the passengers jump out before I turn down to the *chemin de halage*. I drive on, carefully, close to the boat. All four of us lower the putative *perches* to the ground.

It's almost four o'clock. I'm ready to quit. Sam wants to push the tubes together in their telescopic way just to see if they're really long enough and strong enough to do the job. His idea is that we use a rope to pull one of the tubes up onto the boat near a bollard, first. Then with him holding up the other end, standing in the dinghy, we slip one into the other like a giant telescope.

We manipulate the bankside tube into position to slide into the first one. To me, it sounds like a gigantic version of threading a needle, but I can't come up with a better way except to hire a crane or a helicopter.

Pulling the one end up to the front bollard and tying it there isn't too much of a hassle, but now the other end is sunk in the water. Tom, Matt and I slide, pull, bully the bankside tube down the bank so one edge is more or less in line with Sam, who has taken out the little boat and muscled the other end of the tube into the boat with him. I don't even look.

Tom is by the water's edge. He has high boots on. I'm in the middle and Matt's at the top. Sam keeps giving us directions for lining the tubes up. We seem to miss at least twenty times. Then, finally, after what seems hours, but is probably more like five minutes, Sam gives the signal PUSH! and we push like crazy, Sam still giving directions. It reminds me bizarrely of helping my wife have our first baby. And just as with the baby, it suddenly, swiftly, glides in as the baby slid out.

Matt, with our help, pulls the land end up toward the concrete deadman and puts it down near the beams we've pounded in. The telescopic, elongated *perche* is resting on the deadman. Sam gives us instructions to let go so he can see how strong our contraption is; it's obviously long enough.

It doesn't budge. Before we have a chance to cheer, Sam has leaped from the boat and one-handedly pulled himself up onto the *perche,* then swung his leg up so he has the *perche* straddled. Then he stands up on the pole and tightrope walks his way to the bank with a final spring.

"Just like downtown. Couldn't ask for anything better than that, could we? Let's push the other one in place before it's too dark."

At least they could *all* have groaned, but I'm the only one. Sam has moved the dinghy to the rear of the houseboat. Maybe we're getting better or are just lucky, because on about the second trial, we shove that bank tube straight into the boat tube. Sam does his trick again, and we all applaud.

Holes in the "I"s

Monday I drive into Paris to pick up Sam at his parents' boat. He shows me the smaller boat he's built by himself in the space between his parents' boat and the bank. It's beautifully and cleverly designed with a plethora of personal inventions to help him be independent with his missing arm.

He has a good workshop on his boat and most every tool I've ever seen. He's set aside his power drill and some bits as well as everything needed to do some welding. We carry them up to my car. His parents are both working and his sister is in school. We drive through reasonable traffic out to our boat. He says the two of us are enough to do what needs to be done today, but he can't do some things by himself.

We plug in the extension cord, mount a metal bit into his drill and start on the holes in the concrete-bound I-beams. It takes a while for the bits to start penetrating the steel, and Sam stops every few minutes, allowing the steel in the bits to cool so they won't lose their temper. Each hole takes about ten minutes. When he's finished, he shoves the pin through the two holes and has me lift the end of the *perche* over the pin so he can get a good line-up for drilling these holes. He has to give me a hand, his only, but we work it into place. He does some more measuring and marking, then begins drilling with a slightly smaller bit. This goes more quickly, and in five minutes he's finished, drilling straight through from one side to the other. When he comes through the second side, he pulls out the drill and bit, lowers them carefully to the ground, pulls back the welding mask he's been wearing to protect his eyes from flying bits of metal and smiles.

"Now, we can see if our holes are straight."

He stands and straddles the I-beams. I pull out the pin until it's just inside the one I-beam and he grabs it and starts pushing it through the *perche*. It fits fine in the first side, but it's a little off for the second. Sam gets down on his back to check the alignment.

"Give the pin a few taps with the hammer and we'll see if we can force it. It can't be more than a few millimeters off."

I start gently tapping away with the hammer, and it passes through the second side easily.

"Keep hitting it so we can see how it comes out with the other beam. This will be our real test."

I hit with the hammer so the pin slides slowly across to the other beam. I'm hitting lightly, expecting at any minute to hit the solid inside of the beam, but it slips right in without any problem. Sam reaches into his shirt pocket.

"We need to make sure now that the pin stays in place. I brought along two cotter pins. We'll drill holes for them."

He drills those holes. I'm beginning to feel like a woodpecker, only in steel. Sam takes out a small drill and I hold the pin in place while he drills holes into the pin on the outside of each of the beams.

We then go through the entire process again with the bankside pole at the other end of the boat. I'm feeling numb, and I'm only holding or pushing while Sam's doing all the work.

Next, we carry all the equipment onto the boat and start work on the front bollard. Sam has a sort of portable anvil, a vise and a small sledge so we can bend the strap iron into place around the bollard. As usual, it's harder than it looks. Sam is pounding on the other side of the strap iron to bend it round the bollard. He gets them bent to what looks to me as too much.

Then he takes the vise from me and bends the strap back

until he's formed a collar with flat ends coming together on either side of where the boat side of the *perche* is going to be. When he's satisfied with the lineup, he drills holes through the entire conglomerate—easier said than done. Finally, due to Sam's unworldly persistence, we have them all bolted together. This concoction, for sure, isn't going anywhere. Sam is so excited he walks the entire length of the *perche* back to the shore, exactly like a cat or a rat. I wonder where I was when they passed out courage.

We do the back *perche* the same way, finishing off in the dark. This seems to be the way we finish off most days. Rosemary isn't there; it's a school day and Mondays are faculty meetings. I offer to drive Sam back with all his tools, but he decides to leave them on the boat in the front crew cabin.

"We'll need most of this stuff when we work on the chain. I'll need to cut some of it and maybe do some welding. Can you work again tomorrow? It's another one of those jobs I can't do with one hand."

"Look, Sam, I feel terrible about keeping you out of school like this. Aren't you going to get into trouble?"

"If I'm there, I'll probably mess things up with more trouble. I'm not the type for schools. I don't think I'm stupid, but most of the things they teach in a school just don't interest me. I've explained to my dad what I've been doing, and he says he'll sign a paper saying I've been sick. He knows what's important. He didn't used to, but since my accident he's lots better. Mom, of course, being a schoolteacher, twists her nose out of joint, but she isn't going to make any scene. She knows I'm doing the kind of thing I really like to do."

I leave it at that. I wasn't much different in school myself, but he's definitely the most extreme example of the autodidact I've ever known. We call it off for the day, and I'm just ready to drive him up to St.-Germain-en-Laye, when Rosemary and our kids arrive. They're properly impressed with the *perches* and the connection, at least as much as anyone can be impressed if they didn't do it. Matt has all kinds of questions and I begin to feel guilty about sending him off to school when he could be learning along with us.

The Chains That Bind

I drive Sam up to the RER, and on the way he tries explaining his plans for the chain. He's impressed with the weights with which we'll be dealing, and the power we'll need to pull them up into place. He's also worried if the concrete is set enough.

Sam arrives the next morning just as the family is leaving for school. Rosemary asks Sam about school—isn't he going to get into trouble? He tells her to talk with his mom. She knows all about it. Rosemary's in a hurry, they're late already, so she doesn't push it.

Sam and I spend about an hour measuring just how much chain we're going to need. We put the winches in place to attach the front chain. The idea is to pull the chain tight against our *perches*. He says he'll drill holes through the two sections of each *perche* to keep them from telescoping. I'm amazed I understand him the first time. It's almost diabolical the way he has it all worked out.

Sam's still concerned about the weight of the chain, our ability to stack it in the Hillman, and the capability of the Hillman to bear up under the weight. He's also worried about our being able to load and unload the chain ourselves.

"We can always cut our lengths either at Mollard's, or by stretching the chain out on the *berge* here."

We take off for Chez Mollard. We drive all the way to where the chain is stored. Sam goes over to the biggest drum of coiled chain, rolls out about a meter and lifts it in his hand. He hands it to me.

"Here, what do you think this weighs?"

"Heavy, probably ten pounds, and expensive, too, I'll bet."

He goes over to a smaller linked chain. "Well, this is lighter, but I don't think you could be absolutely sure it would hold under pressure. That's a big, heavy boat, and the water can be fast and hard."

He pulls out his list of measurements. It includes the distance from both front bollard to deadman and back bollard to deadman. Also, there are the long pieces from front bollard to back deadman and from back bollard to front deadman, crossing in the middle. It comes to sixty-five meters.

We find the yard man and ask him what the cost per meter is. He shrugs his shoulders and points up to the front office. What a dumb way to sell things. Sam and I trudge up to the office. Sam explains what we want. We're given a per-meter figure that isn't too scary, but multiplied by sixty-five is more than significant.

"Well, Sam, we'll be eating beans around our house for a while, but OK. Here we go again."

Sam smiles and we order. I stay to pay with my magic empty card and Sam goes back to the yard, running.

When I come out, there's chain spread all over the yard. Sam is checking measurements and straightening out the chain. The yard man is standing with a pair of long-handled nippers by the drum of chain. Sam whispers to me.

"I couldn't get the jerk to cut off any chain until he'd seen the invoice stamped. But I've talked him into doing our cutting for us. I hope our measurements are right."

I hand the invoice to Sam and he hands it to the yard man. He smiles and nips off from the drum. The chain is beautiful and, in a certain way, frightening. Maybe it has to do with being chained up on a chain gang or chained into the dungeon of a French prison in some other life.

Sam starts running along, pulling the lengths of chain taut and marking the links we want cut. Just straightening out that chain on the ground is a test of strength. But finally we have them all cut.

We start coiling them to load into the Hillman. Come on, brave Husky, little Hillman, one more time, please. Sam's convinced that if we distribute the weight right, we can take all the chain in one load. So, somehow, we stack it all in, large coils of bright silver-colored chain. Sam does his shock test on the back bumper, then the front, shakes his head but smiles.

"Now we need links that will open to hold the chain around the bollards and the I-beams."

He measures one link of chain, then talks with the yard man. The separate, opening links are sold in another part of the yard. It's more of a hardware section. The front of the car is tilted up like a motorboat going through the water fast, but we're not going *anywhere* fast.

We need eight of these opening links. Sam describes what we need to a heavy man wearing thick glasses. He stares at Sam's missing arm. He comes back with a wooden box filled with chain-link connectors.

Sam pulls out one and measures it. He smiles at me. He talks to the fat man and writes out just what we're buying for me to present to the office. Here we go again.

These little devils turn out to be expensive but, as usual, there's no turning back. We give the guy the stamped invoice and he puts the missing links into a small cardboard box for us. We add our new acquisitions to the weight in the car.

I don't go more than fifteen kilometers an hour all the way through Le Pecq and into Port Marly. Sam keeps leaning out the car and motioning people to pass us. For the first time, I have some sympathy for the drivers of tractors pulling trailers filled with hay down at the mill in the country. I just smile at people as they go by with scowling faces. I don't go more than five Ks per hour down the *chemin de halage*, with Sam out in front directing me around potholes and bumps. I'm dripping nervous sweat when we finally pull up in front of the boat.

We tug and pull one of the shorter chains out of the car. We spread it along the *berge* from deadman to the edge of the water. Sam looks at the length of chain and the coiled end by the water.

"This is a job for you. Take the length of rope from the inside of your car, walk out onto the boat to that bollard up there and throw one end of the rope to me. I'll wait here."

I do all that, and Sam catches the end of the rope, first time, with his one arm. He stoops and ties a fancy, one-handed knot through the last link of the chain. I pull on the rope and bring the chain up the side of the boat. I wrap it twice around the bollard.

"OK, hold it there while I go hook the winch onto the other end of the chain."

He's already dashing up the hill of the *berge*. I watch him up at the deadman. He wraps the chain around the two I-beams and below the *perche* attachment. He scrambles to the car and brings down the box with the chain-link attachments. He threads it over the end link, then over another link close to the I-beams. He twists the tightener of this linking link with his fingers and finally with a pair of pliers he has in his back pocket.

Then he runs along the *chemin de halage,* across the gangplank back onto the boat. We pull together until we have the chain as tight as we can. Then he hooks the winch onto the chain at one end and the other end onto one of the braces holding the bollard. We start cranking and keep pulling till the chain is taut. Then Sam hooks the linking link from the first link past the winch to the nearest part of the extended chain. We then uncrank the winch and the chain goes taut against the tie on land. Sam takes off to check the tie there and the condition of the deadman. He shouts across the water.

"It's great, didn't budge an inch. Let's try the other one now."

We go through the same gyrations as we connect the front bollard to the front deadman. I'm pulling, breaking a gut, and thinking of those longer cross chains lying along the *berge.* That's going to be something.

But we do manage, with Sam at the front end and me at the back, each with a winch. We alternately tighten till Sam feels we have the boat even against the bank and not so far in we can't see up and down the river. He crawls out on the *perche* to drill and drive in the pins to stabilize the telescoped *perches*. I think of how I tugged and struggled, digging in the river, slipping and sliding up the bank, cranking that damned winch, trying for every centimeter, and here we are moving the whole boat around as if it were nothing.

It's the same procedure, putting in the cross chains, only the weight is much greater. I'm content with what we already have, I'm not really into overkill, but I'm learning. The river is a great teacher. Sam's at the back deadman and has the chain already hooked. I'm on deck at the front cranking on the winch. The slack in the chain is being taken up, and my arms, shoulders and back are about to break. Sam comes running up to join me. He starts cranking with me.

"We've got to be careful the thin cables on the winch don't break. If they do, we can be cut in half."

He doesn't offer any solutions to avoid this decapitation, or worse, so I just tuck my head in close between my shoulders. Sam is cranking away with me, using his foot for additional strength on the handle of the winch.

At last, Sam feels the chain is as tight as we should pull it until we have the other chain in place. Without a break, we start on that one. I feel as though I'm paralyzed along my whole right side and my kidneys are about to burst through my ribs. I straighten up slowly and practically crawl over to the back bollard and the other winch. Sam hooks the chain to the front deadman the same way as the others. I'm beginning to see why he wanted so much concrete in the deadman. This boat is pulling against itself!

I start cranking. Sam is running back and forth, deadman to deadman, bollard to bollard, walking out on the *perches,* checking

159

the length and tension on the chains. I'm cranking and cursing. Sam comes to help as we crank this chain right up to touch our first cross chain. He taps me on the shoulder to stop me. My whole shoulder is practically paralyzed anyway. I slump onto my rump, sweat pouring out of me. My whole face is wet with it, and this is genuine sweat. My face is so wet it feels as if I've been crying. Maybe I was. But I look at the chains, neat and straight as threads on a loom. Sam is like a madman. He hangs on each of the chains while he stands on the bank. I know if he had two hands, he'd hand-over-hand it onto the boat. He's smiling.

"Well, we really did it. This might be the best moored boat on the river. You could play a tune on those chains."

CHAPTER XVI

10-Meter I-Beams

NOW WITH THE houseboat securely moored, and the gangplank firmly in place, I feel we can relax and begin to enjoy our boat. And that turns out to be the case, although I have no idea of all the work that still needs to be done.

Living with a houseboat is like living with a demanding woman. Each time you think there's a chance for peace and quiet, to read a newspaper, or perhaps think or dream, something else wrong comes to light. In our case, only two weeks after we've finished rectifying the damage done by the flood, family complaints are being lodged regarding the steadiness of the gangplank. It bounces.

Of course, for me, that gangplank, and all the work it represents, is like my child. I try not to be too defensive, but Rosemary and the girls demonstrate how they need to walk across one at a time or they'll be bounced off. I hadn't thought of that.

So Matt and I decide the only solution is to put two ten-meter lengths of I-beam from the boat to the *chemin de halage*. There's no way we can carry these, so we ask for delivery. Luckily, again, my guardian angels—that is, my buyers—have already sprung to my defense, and I've sold eleven more paintings, some of which actually have a physical reality, although six are still only more phantom paintings. I know they're all going to be paintings of the river and the boats along it. It's what I want to do. Also, the paintings I've sent back have made quite a sensation with my limited clientele, and they're asking for more of the same. So, in painting sales alone, the boat is beginning to pay off—although it swallows the money almost as fast as it attracts it.

Matt wants us, just the two of us, to do this operation; this is a family matter. I'm dubious. I haven't yet dealt with any I-beams over two meters long, and even *they* were heavy. Matt says he has it all worked out. I think he's emulating Sam, but he doesn't have Sam's experience. I figure as long as we can keep one end of an I-beam on land, we won't lose it in the water, and we can always appeal for help.

The day arrives. A huge delivery truck from Chez Mollard comes with the I-beams. It has a special carrier built along one side of the truck and up past the driver's seat to carry them, along with other long metal pieces. The driver blazes his way through the Le Clercs' poor willow trees and pulls up beside us. The driver's a short, compact man wearing dirty French working-blues. He has large, dirt-impacted hands. Metal gives off a black residue that seems to invade everything.

He climbs down from his high perch and looks across at the boat. Matt explains to him what we want. He goes through a series of hand motions, reminiscent of *les frères Teurnier,* with which I presume he's trying to explain his system for mounting the I-beams. The guy shrugs. He goes back to his truck and unties our beams. My God! They're enormous. I think even Matt's somewhat intimidated. We pull them off and stretch them along the *chemin de halage.* I can't imagine how we're going to span that gulf, across water, without heavy equipment. We can, all three of us, just barely pull them from the truck. I have no pride. I ask Matt to see if this short, stocky guy has any idea how we can put these monsters in place. Matt's nose is bent out of shape because I don't have confidence in him.

This burly brute just jams his hands on his hips, akimbo, I think it's called. He purses his lips in and out a few times. Then he points at a large rock imbedded in the *berge* just at the edge of the *chemin de halage*. Under his direction, we swing one of the I-beams so it spins on top of this rock. This calls for much pushing, grunting, sweating and cursing on our part, and shouted instructions from the driver. He's pushing, grunting, sweating and cursing along with us.

Matt runs across the gangplank and comes out of the boat with a rope. The driver and I have all our weight on the land end of the I-beam, just holding it in place, keeping it balanced on the rock. Matt slips the rope over the boat end of the beam and wraps it on the same bollard we used to tie up the gangplank. We, the driver and I, keep pushing at Matt's signal, a little at a time, until Matt can pull that end over the edge of the upper boat. Matt's pleased as a little boy; so am I, and so's the driver.

He starts explaining in fast French what we should do with the second I-beam. I pick up only part of it, but Matt seems satisfied. The driver brings out the invoice for me to sign. I reach in my pocket for some change as Matt runs into the boat. I'm trying to force the driver to take twenty francs, when Matt comes out with a bottle of red wine, not the best, but better than ordinary table wine, *vin ordinaire*. Matt holds it out to him as he races cross the gangplank. This he'll take, and with a smile.

Then he puts up a hand and goes back to his truck. He returns with two small pieces of I-beam about a foot long each. He explains to Matt how we're to use them. We shake hands all around and then guide him back down the *chemin de halage* through the trees. This is quite a trick, but I imagine it's duck soup compared to many of the deliveries he makes.

Matt explains to me what we need to do with the second I-beam. It seems simple enough, but I'm not convinced we can do it without the know-how and probably ninety kilos of pure muscle from the truck driver. The idea is to swing the beam around the same as we did the first time, then slide it out on top of the I-beam already in place. It sounds simple enough and, despite my reservations, it turns out not to be beyond our strength or ability.

After securing the boat ends of the I-beams, we slide the land ends to the edge of the gangplank. We lift the gangplank, using the heavy metal ladder as a lever, and slide the two I-beams under the gangplank, one on a side.

Then we go up onto the boat bringing my auto jack with us. Now we check out the truck driver's idea. We jack up the ends of the I beams there on the boat, and slide under each of them those small bits of I-beams the driver'd given us. They prove much more than an even exchange for the wine. It brings the end of the gangplank right up even with the door. I swear it looks as if we planned it. We retie the wooden gangplank to the bollards, and everything is tight and secure.

Matt and I go inside, our shirts drenched with sweat, and each open a bottle of Kronenberg 64 beer. Matt hardly ever drinks beer. We come out again and walk back and forth over our now-solid gangplank. It's been a big achievement for each of us. It's been a day Matt could well afford to miss school.

When the girls come home, they're thrilled. They walk up and down the gangplank the way we did, even jumping. They try all three of them at once. It's still steady. Matt and I watch with pride.

Massive Mahogany

Other projects keep coming up, and we do them one at a time, as we can. But I can paint now. I start painting up and down the river, pedaling on my bicycle with the paintbox and canvas on my back. Not only is the river beautiful, but all the little western suburban towns have nooks and corners, old buildings, just begging to be painted. The Impressionists knew what they were doing. With this kind of material, one can hardly miss. I'm painting better and more than I ever did in Paris.

One of my first non-painting projects on the boat, which isn't exactly an emergency, is to build a big desk. In Paris, I've found a place where they have huge, thick slabs of mahogany shipped in on enormous trucks, most of them from Africa. Then they cut them in thin layers to use as veneer on furniture. It could break your heart.

After selling five more paintings, I make a bid on one piece of wood, solid mahogany, six centimeters thick, three meters long and a meter wide! I buy it for only seventy dollars. There's a slight crack in it, so they give it to me for about half the regular price. They say they've never actually sold any of this wood directly to someone who doesn't want to slice it like cheese. I ask if they'll split it down the middle so I have two three-centimeter pieces. They do it with incredibly big band saws. It's a sacrilege to cut it, but I could never manage with the full thick slab.

The Hillman isn't Husky enough for this job. I go in on a Saturday morning and, with the workers' help, hoist it up onto the roof rack of the Simca and tie it down. They estimate it weighs more than a hundred and fifty kilos (over three hundred pounds).

I drive slowly the width of Paris from east to west, then another seventeen kilometers out to the boat, the same distance Rosemary and the kids had been doing before we fixed up the boat. I'm wondering all the time how Matt and I will manage to haul all this off the car and down into the hull of the boat. I've already done the measuring; it will fit down through the staircase, but at an angle and *juste*.

Matt's waiting for me. He's already called Tom, but Tom was working on preparing for some exam. Matt wants to see if we can do this just ourselves, again.

When we try to lift the wood, I'm really glad I had it cut in two. There's no way we could've maneuvered the original six centimeters over that gangplank. Even with all the I-beams, it might have dumped us into the water.

Carefully we push it through the front door of the upper boat, tilting it to turn the corner and down the steps. I'm hoping my measurements are right, and they are, *juste*. That seems to be my style, *juste*. We have the first piece positioned, finally, at the top of the steps. I duck under it and squeeze through to the bottom. Matt holds tight while I take the weight of it, and we slide it down the steps one at a time. It's a really tight squeeze, but we do it. I'm ready to quit, but Matt says let's get it over with while we're in the swing of things. God, YOUTH!

When they're both down there, we spread them out in what will be the studio when I'm finished. I still haven't put the *frisette* ceiling on the back room. This should be a good place to work. I show Matt my plans for making a U-shaped desk using no nails. He's excited, too. The idea is to make the supports of solid pieces fitted into each other the way the old egg-crate boxes were. That is, we cut vertical cuts in the middle and halfway through each piece and slide them tight over each other. It sounds complicated and it is, but it works. First, we portion out what's to be the top of the desk, with about a three-foot wraparound on each side, then cut the four beautiful, deep, redwood panels to make the supports. We come out with just the amount of wood we need, virtually no waste. I'm beginning to feel I'm not such a klutz after all.

When we put it together, we fasten all the joints and intersections with dowling. We rent the hand sander and get the top smooth. The natural grain of the wood begins to show. When we have it waxed and finished, it isn't perfect, but it's a beautiful piece of sculpture. It took us two weeks, but Matt had school many of those days, and this slowed us down.

I put my typewriter storage boxes and an extra phone I found in an abandoned boat down river onto the desk and begin to feel like a big-shot businessman. It's to be a desk everybody can use for homework, grading papers or whatever. We set it up at the very back of the bottom boat.

Time Flies

This gives some idea of the kinds of things we do to make the boat a really special place to live. Another time, there's a *brocante* sale on the island about three kilometers from the boat, sort of a flea market. I go and fall in love with wall clocks, something the French, at that time, seem to think are useless and a nuisance. Why wind a clock when one can have a nice electric clock that doesn't tick and doesn't chime?

I buy seven of these clocks, as well as a grandfather job. I spend time between painting, cleaning and fixing these up, finding missing pieces at a shop in Paris and then varnishing the outside of the clocks.

I get all seven of them going at once, down in the hull. I have them set just a bit off each other so they sing in sequence. I learn to adjust the timing by lengthening or shortening the pendulum. After a week of clocks dinging and donging frantically, on the quarter hour, practically all the time, the family revolts. It's decided I can run only one at a time, plus the grandfather clock in the living room upstairs.

Then there's the rug scene. Despite all my scrounging around for rugs at *Abbé Pierre's*, the rugs are a bit dingy. It's like that—when everything is a mess, everything *new* looks good, but when it's fixed up, they begin to seem more shabby all the time.

There's an advertisement in the school newspaper for a washing machine and dryer. We haven't had anything like that since we left the States. The price is right. An IBM manager is going back to the States, and IBM has decided that although these machines are still working, they aren't worth shipping back. We call immediately and make arrangements to see them. They're wonderful and we buy them. The plan is to keep them out on the front deck with a removable cover. Rosemary is absolutely tickled; in Paris there were several Laundromats nearby, but out here in the suburbs there are not so many, and they're all far away from the boat.

CHAPTER XVII

The Rug Merchants, Part I

I'M DELIVERING A painting to an American woman in Saint-Cloud. She and her family are being shipped back home and want to take something of Paris with them.

I'm walking around admiring the rugs in her beautiful apartment. They're the kind you almost need to lift your feet not to trip over, heavy, thick, deep brown. The woman sees me looking.

"IBM only allows us so much weight and we're never going to fit these into the weight limit. We've investigated and found it would cost a fortune to ship them ourselves. Do you think you'd like to buy them?"

Sure I would. Then I could paint for the rest of my life trying to pay *this* bill off.

"They're certainly beautiful."

"They're wool, practically brand new, and have rubber bubbled lining under them. Feel it."

I kneel down to feel. I've never felt rugs like these, and they're wall-to-wall through the entire apartment, bedrooms, closets, the whole place.

"I don't think we can ever afford anything like this, but it is really tempting. We live on a boat, you know, and the cold seems to come in from everywhere, especially up under our feet."

"Let me ask Bill. I think I'll change to lighter colors when we're back in Boca Raton. Florida is different than France, you know."

Yep, I know. France is better. She leaves and goes to another part of the house. She comes back.

"Bill says you can have all the rugs if you'll wait until the day we move, then move them out yourselves. He says that under those conditions, he'll let you have them for two thousand francs."

I can't believe it. I want to go right out and start painting.

"That's certainly generous of you. Are you sure?"

She was sure. They were sure.

And so we buy this beautiful rug. I can't believe it. We're going to live like millionaires. I'll roll around on that soft rug at night and all I'll need is some soft stereo music playing. I should look in that school newspaper to see if anybody is switching from records to tapes or tapes to cassettes and I can buy their beautiful, low-tech music. I'm going crazy. When I tell her, Rosemary looks, staring at me as if she's looking for definite signs of insanity.

We promise to have the check for the rug as soon as possible. They're moving just before we go down to the mill, but I'm not going to wait that long to give her the check. She might just come to her senses. Then I'd *really* go crazy, walking around on hard floors.

Canaries

While waiting for the big rug day, I'm running in circles, figuring where to put all this beautiful liner and rug. I also begin thinking about my canary aviary. It will be four meters wide, two meters deep and three meters high. The birds would love a carpet like this, too, soft as grass, but it'd be hard to clean. I hate keeping creatures in captivity, but birds in an aviary like this could really fly; they probably won't notice they're in a cage. I start calculating the cost of materials and canaries. I can hear them singing. It will be beautiful, better than any stereo.

I do a double-mesh cage with dark-green half-centimeter-square, plastic-covered wire. I build the frame for the cage with French two-by-fours and place them two feet apart. I finish the frame with a dark oak stain. I build a small hobbitlike door I can just squeeze into on the land side of the cage. I double-mesh in the ceiling, too, for safety.

Over the top of this, I lay clear corrugated plastic with the corrugations facing toward the rear of the boat to run off the water.

The floor of the cage I line with Astroturf. It will complicate cleaning the cage but makes it more natural; the green is as good an imitation of natural grass as I'm going to find. I thought of planting grass sod on the floor, but this would be impossible to clean, even if it grew.

The back window of our bedroom opens directly into the cage, and I build a platform just outside where I can put feeders and waterers I buy in the bird market. Later, I intend to find a large cement garden bowl and keep it aerated and filled with water from a small fountain. I do finally do that, too. I'm going overboard, almost literally, but this is something I've always wanted.

Sundays, in Paris, the flower market is converted to a bird market where anyone who has birds for sale or is interested in buying a bird, or who just likes birds, comes.

It's a place I've always enjoyed visiting. Now I have an excuse and a reason. I'm interested in birdsong; not color, not size, not flying. I want to hear beautiful birdsong on my boat in the river. I ask around all the bird dealers and amateurs who have birds to sell. I finally decide to invest in one of the best canary breeds for song, in France, the Malinoise. These are a radiant yellow, usually with one dark spot somewhere on the head.

Since I'm making the big investment, I look only at birds that have been in song competitions and have scorecards, like pedigrees for dogs. These cards show their songs and their scores in all the various kinds of singing arias expected of this breed. There are over twenty different arias to be evaluated, and points are given for each. The highest total score I see is ninety-six, but, for reasons of my own, reasons I can't even define, I don't like this bird. But there is a bird with a score of seventy-six who sings every time I pass by, and I swear he's singing right to me. After listening to him three Sundays in a row, I buy him. I don't tell Rosemary how much I pay for this bird. Each of us has a *folie.*

I buy a special seed mix for Malinoise canaries, along with cuttlefish bone, gravel for his crop, some health food and special feeders and waterers to put on the shelf outside our window. I also buy a book on raising Malinoise canaries.

When I turn him loose in the cage, leaning through the bedroom window, my heart's in my mouth. What if I didn't find and close all the possible places he can escape? What if cats can somehow grab him through the mesh? I'm a nervous wreck.

Then he starts singing. He sings as if he sees the lovely flowing river, the spring trees coming into bloom, the beautiful French sky with the moving, expanding, billowing French clouds. I know he's an artist bird. I leave the window open and stretch out on the bed. Soft winds waft his song to me, and I'm no longer nervous. This is better than any Valium. This is better than any other kind of music.

The Rug Merchant,
Part II

Then the day comes to go fetch the carpet. The owners are moving out on Sunday, and they want the carpet removed on Saturday after all the furniture has been packed and hauled away. Saturday's great because Matt and Tom have the day off from school, although final exams are coming up.

We pull up in front of the apartment with the Simca. Their children see us from the third floor and wave; one comes down to let us in. We shake hands all around, and the lady of the house is crying. She really doesn't want to leave France, even for Boca Raton. The apartment looks immense now without the furniture, and those carpets seem to stretch all the way to the horizon.

We check the places where the men who laid the carpet have made the joinings, and we loosen them. They've used the kind of tape that's glued on both sides to hold the carpet down. We decide to take out one of the bedroom carpets first. We line up on the wall under the window and start to roll. Already I can see this verges on the impossible. How can rugs be so heavy? We tilt the roll up and muscle it into the hall. We're looking at each other and wondering. Even the rubber underliner is no lightweight. I'm amazed the floors of this place didn't cave in. My boat will be sitting several centimeters deeper in the water, that is if we can ever actually push and pull these big babies into the boat.

After much struggle, discovering we can't force the carpet through the door and down the elevator, we elect to push it out the window. We stagger with one rolled rug over to the balcony and lift it onto the railing. My job is to go downstairs and warn anybody who might be coming in or out the door to stop, and then give the signal to let her fly!

I wait down there till all's clear, then yell and wave my arm. They push. The roll of rug comes down faster than I thought. I almost don't get out of the way, and it makes an enormous thump when it hits. Several people appear on different balconies of the building, looking concerned. We smile and try to ignore them. Then, one, two, three, we swing and roll the rug up onto the roof of the car. We're all pooped.

I'm beginning to have my usual feeling that I've bitten off more than I can chew. Also, I'm wondering how these rugs were lifted *up* into the apartment. It must have been done by some kind of piano movers. We tie the rug on tight, then go up for the second rug. We take the elevator up.

The rest of the rugs, three bedrooms and a hall's worth, we get up and out about the same way. It's obvious we're ignoring the monster, that brown landing field of a rug in the living room. We don't want to hold up these nice people, who are moving back to Boca Raton, any longer than necessary, so each trip to the boat, we leave the rugs rolled up on the gangplank. This must be the ultimate test for those beams and I-beams. It takes three different trips to haul them there. I'm beginning to think of carpeting the *chemin de halage* outside our boat as well, just to use up all this rug.

When we start rolling the big rug, it becomes apparent we have another set of problems. One, the roll of rug is so huge, I'm not sure the three of us can lift it at all, let alone lift it up onto the railing of the balcony. I'm not even sure we can push it through the sliding doors out to the balcony. Then, I hate to think of what happens when it hits. Maybe someone will phone an ambulance or the fire department or the police. We might set off earthquake alarms.

After much head scratching and staring down at this solid tube of wool and whatever it is the wool is woven into, we decide our only chance is for the three of us to yank and pull till we have one end up on the balcony railing. Then we'll all push until we've reached the middle of the carpet roll, hoping the rail won't collapse. I'll run down and warn the local populace that the sky is about to fall in. They'll turn the rug on a pivot and shove as hard as they can so as to clear the balcony below. We can't think of anything else. It's something like the problem Matt and I had with the I-beams, only worse.

But, somehow we do it, just clearing the second-floor balcony.

Thank God, nobody was sticking a head out down there, leaning over the railing to see what all the ruckus is about, or the head would have been sheared off and buried under a quarter-ton of carpet.

When we're finished, we're all sweaty, dust-covered and mostly very shaky from exhaustion. The Goodwins, the people from whom we've bought the carpet, invite us up for a can of beer. He's smiling and she's still crying. The apartment seems *really* empty now. He looks around.

"Ever since we sold this to you, I've been wondering how you intended to maneuver it out of here. I thought you'd have a professional team of movers, and even then I couldn't think how they'd do it. I wasn't here when it was put in; we didn't move any furniture in until the carpet was laid. You guys are crazy."

Well, on that last part he's definitely right. And this was the easy end of the job. Now we need to work it out onto the boat. I won't bother going into the details of that, except to say we measure and cut pieces to fit out on the *chemin de halage* before we try to muscle it in. We pass the large piece for the downstairs rooms into the dinghy and through the large window in back, just over the new desk. Again, it looks as if we planned it. It's enough to encourage someone into believing there's a power greater than all of us that takes care of over-ambitious fools, like race car drivers, hot dog skiers, ultralight-plane fliers and people who move rugs weighing too much. By the way, the boat doesn't sink a centimeter.

Of course, we don't always make our cuts and measurements right, so there's much trimming to do. I buy three rug-cutting knives at the hardware store in Le Pecq along with a sharpening stone. After two days, we're fairly good at estimating and cutting. One of our major problems is shifting the big pieces of rug around in the two large downstairs rooms, along with the rubber rug liners. The liners are too bulky to push down the inside stairs, so we're wrestling them through that back window, too. There are a few times I think we're going to carpet the bottom of the Seine, but in the end, it works out. It's five in the afternoon of the second day when we finish. I pull a six-pack out of the refrigerator, and we sit around the table in the living room. The table's still somewhat wobbly from missing glue but has served the purpose. We don't talk too much because we're out of breath and energy.

I notice Matt leaning back in his chair against the river side of the boat where the original fire had been. He looks one way, then the other.

"Dad, think about how great it would be if we had a bay window right here so we could look up and down the river."

Tom and I look at him as if he's kidding. A bay window on a boat? But then, that original window right there never did really recover from the fire. It's held together with wood putty, staples and glue. I start to laugh. Tom and Matt look as if I've gone mad. I'm thinking maybe they're right.

Creative Life and Dancing

The houseboat seems very conducive to me for creative work. There's something about being separate from the land, being alone, having the big desk and a quiet place to work. I also have a set of filing cabinets I bought at *Abbé Pierre's*. I find that working on this boat seems to open up blocks based on confusion and a sense of being scattered all over the landscape. I bear down and write two books within three years. One of them is published by a major publisher, and I have an advance on it equal to ten paintings. When the paperback sale comes in, we have the kind of money that lets us consider not selling paintings anymore at all, just paint and use the money to buy materials. I'm playing Theo to my own Vincent. I've never had life so good.

Rosemary likes teaching, and I can't convince her to quit and do whatever it is she wants, but she insists teaching kindergarten is exactly what she really wants to do. There's still the problem of the enormous tuitions for our children at the American School, which we'd need to pay if she quit. The paperback sale isn't for *that* kind of money.

The day I sign the contract for the paperback, we decide to celebrate by having the dance party we'd promised way back when we were nailing floorboards with Neil, Barbara, Robin, Donna and Jo. We roll up the rug in the back section of the boat, pile it on top of my desk to protect everything, borrow the sound system from the school so we can have loud music. I photocopy an invitation to all of Rosemary's kindergarten parents, most of our friends on the faculty, and a few other non–school related friends.

The invitation tells them there will be a dance on the boat. We'll supply the music, wine and beer. Each person is encouraged to bring something to share around. If they want to enlarge our wine and beer supply, that's also welcome, but no hard liquor. Also, and, especially, no smoking except on the front deck of the boat.

The night of the dance, I run around town putting up arrows and signs to help people find the boat. We've invited about seventy guests, expecting maybe twenty. Over eighty arrive. Luckily, the gangplank is strong, and the boat has two stories. I also put no smoking signs all over the boat with a cigarette-cum-arrow pointing to the front deck. I've covered the deck with Astroturf and put some extra chairs out there, so it's a comfortable place to kill yourself.

The way it works out, without any actual planning on our part, is that in the living room, where we have a small fire burning in an open Franklin stove we've installed, we have what I call the philosophers' corner. This attracts the kinds of people who like to sit around at a party and talk, solving the problems of the world and laying their own problems on each other. They're also close to the front door so they can go out to smoke whenever the spirit or addiction hits them. The deck party is not just smokers but people who want to talk, often pulled from the philosophers' corner, and those young of heart who want a nice dark place. I try not to worry about people falling off the boat, but I remind all of them about the life preservers, just in case.

Downstairs, at the foot of the stairs, we set up tables on which we spread out the food as it arrives. We keep a steady running supply of pizzas coming from the small oven in our kitchen. It's to fill in any empty spaces, but there never are any; there's more food than anybody could ever eat. This is more of a gourmand cocktail party.

People stand around and chat or gossip or whatever while drinking and eating. This part of the party is where my ladder-staircase comes down and is usually jammed chock-full. There, we have adequate but not bright electric light, enough to see with whom you're speaking and what you're drinking or eating.

In the back section downstairs, where we've rolled up the rug, we have the dance party. There's all kinds of dancing. We've asked special friends to bring tapes of the kind of dance music they like. Back there with the music and the darkness, it usually starts slowly, but by ten o'clock it's a regular discotheque. It's my favorite part of the party.

I dance with everybody. Rosemary likes to dance, too, and between pulling pizzas out of the oven, we dance down there. I have my little wrist alarm set at twenty minutes for each pizza. Here, the only light is from candles in wine bottles. It's very romantic and everybody dances with everybody. No discotheque ever was as jumping as this is. The entire boat gets to rocking; one can feel the swaying and rocking from front to back.

One rule in France is that if you're going to give a party, and you can give only one party a month, you must notify your neighbors a week ahead of time, then close it down, at least the loud music, by two A.M. It's also considered good form to invite immediate neighbors to the party. A party such as ours is called by the French, a *"boom."*

We warn everybody both in the invitation and through the night that the party will shut down at two, promptly. Rosemary and I are not young, and the cleanup is a big job, so at five minutes to two, we blink the lights and come down with plastic sacks. We encourage everyone to put their plastic cups, paper plates and so forth in one sack and their bottles in another. We also remind everyone to gather up their dishes or pans in which they've brought food. Some heed these requests, while others are more recalcitrant. Rosemary keeps a subtle watch for those who participate or reciprocate, and those who don't. At two, I start blowing out candles and turn off the music.

At the first party there was much moaning and groaning, but then as we gave more parties, gradually eliminating the recalcitrant from the invitations, things go like clockwork, literally. We can be in bed by two-thirty, with the place cleaned up, rug rolled in place and everything back to normal.

The only trouble is the constant demand for more parties. We begin to feel we're running a commercial discotheque, so we make the parties seasonal, one for spring, one for end of summer, one for fall (costume) and one for winter. These parties have been going on for many years now and are one of the fun parts of living on the boat. As they grow up, our children join the parties and the dancing, and come to know their teachers in a way they never would have. Rosemary also likes having all the mothers and fathers of her little kindergartners there. Many new friendships are struck up between these people with similar situations and interests. The boat becomes a real social center for Americans living in Paris.

A Marriage on the River

The best party we ever have on the boat is a family one. Our oldest daughter, Kate, decides she wants to marry a wonderful man with whom she's teaching at an international school in Munich. His name is Bill.

Neither of them wants an ordinary marriage. In fact, they want to be married on the boat. Most of Bill's family from Oregon have never been east of the Rockies or west of Puget Sound. But they're all coming. I'm glad we have those thick rugs in the rooms downstairs. We borrow sleeping bags from everywhere.

We set up the area for the marriage with the window looking out on the Seine behind the bride and groom. Jo, my painting buddy with whom I share a studio in Paris, marries them. He does a very moving ceremony with much compassion and wisdom. He's been a family friend since Kate was a little girl. He has five children of his own, about the age of ours.

We play a tape of Mendelssohn's wedding march. Everyone is sitting on the floor all over the upper boat. We drink champagne and then prepare for the fun part. Today is the first of November. This is the birthday and wedding anniversary of Rosemary's sister Emmaline. She's been dead several years at the time of this wedding.

The dance is a Halloween-like costume affair and there is much wild dancing and stomping. I begin to worry about those boards we nailed in so casually, but there's no problem. However, what with all the drinking champagne, beer and wine, nobody falls off the boat.

Now that Kate and Bill and their two babies are gone, killed by a combination of greed and cupidity under an eighteen-wheeler truck in the smoke of fieldgrass burning in Oregon, we can begin to look back on that wonderful moment and rejoice for them.

It's been more than five years since we lost this large part of our family, and the emptiness will always be there, but in our grief, it's been healing to have those poignant memories of their wedding, the madhouse, the fun, the laughter, the confidence in continuity. Somehow, their having been married on the boat made the entire pattern of their brief lives make some sense.

CHAPTER XVIII

A Wonderful Surprise

ABOUT THREE YEARS after the wedding, after traveling for the summer, we come home to find that Sam and Matt, along with Camille, Tom and some other friends, have fulfilled Matt's wish about a bay window. They really *did* it. I'm glad I wasn't even around to watch this project. I'd probably have had apoplexy.

We had no idea what they were planning. Under Sam's direction, first they push out the wall of the living room and kitchen to the edge of the boat, extending the floor, roof, ceiling, everything, more than half a meter. With the wall, they've moved the big plate-glass window. Then they put in multipaned windows across the new, enlarged kitchen. They've built Matt's bay window in the living room, out yet another half-meter over the river with six interlocking, hinged, glass multipaned doors from floor to ceiling. It makes a perfect bay in which we can put the dining table and chairs so they don't block the way in the living room. It would have been a great place to have had the wedding ceremony. Now, as Matt said, we can really see up- and downriver wonderfully.

They've built new cabinets in the kitchen, put in a new gas stove and, miracle of miracles, a beautiful refrigerator and freezer. There's also a stainless steel drainboard with two sinks. Such luxury, like something out of *House & Garden,* or maybe that should be *Houseboats & River.* Also, hidden under the drainboard is a dishwasher. This is something we've never had, or thought we ever would have.

When we come back from our trip, they're all there excited and celebrating. What a great christening party we have for the new boat. It's hard to believe. Rosemary goes from one room to the other, trying to adjust herself to the additional space, especially the kitchen.

They've put in a new ceiling joist to span the section that had been resting on the wall before, and they've used two posts to hold the weight. The engineering is definitely Sam's. The bay windows open directly out over the Seine itself. The entire bay window is cantilevered. It looks like a fine place to dive from, if they ever get the Seine as clean as they say they're going to, or it could be a convenient suicide jump.

Rosemary's Retirement

Rosemary comes to a point where she has only one more year to teach. Then, by French law she must retire. In France, like it or not, the year you turn sixty-five, you must retire. She fights it, but it's no use. The *Ministre de Travail* knows his rules, and there can be no exceptions. At first, Rosemary is very put out, and so is super-mothering this last nest of kindergartners through the year. She says it's the best class she's ever had, but I can't remember a year when she didn't say the same thing.

She's setting up a sort of kindergartner alumni association of all those she's taught over the past twenty-two years. She searches out addresses and consults her own records. Some of these kindergartners are almost thirty years old now. What she wants most is to have a place of her own on the boat as an office, a place to carry out her kindergarten alumni plans, and to write. Her idea is to have it in the place where I've built my aviary.

During the last twenty-five years, I've been raising my wonderful singing birds. At times I've had over fifty birds in that aviary. It's my pride and joy. But the birds do hold us down. Each time we leave for the mill or to travel, we need to find someone who will care for them. Also, because they've inbred for so long, I'm beginning to have empty nests, empty eggs and birds that don't do their jobs as parents, won't feed the young, so they die.

I agree that Rosemary should have her office. I think about putting the birds in smaller cages or maybe letting them fly free and just keep putting out food for them in a feeder on the roof until they lose out in the battle for survival in the big world. This last solution fits my feelings better about captive animals. I build the feeding station and let the birds go. It's late summer and they stay around the boat, singing in the trees, flashes of yellow against the green, flying their wonderful undulating flight and learning to avoid magpies, hawks, cats and all the dangers of the free life for a song bird.

Sam and I take down the aviary. Sam has wonderful plans. He's graduated from high school now and has married our second daughter, Camille. Who knows how many lives this boat has affected?

He spends three days down at my desk drawing. What he shows me when he's finished is almost an entirely different boat. Rosemary has given him all the input as to what she wants in her office. This includes big windows looking out on the river, with a large desk under the window, small, clerestory windows on the side facing our upriver boat neighbor, a large closet all the way across on the land side. Sam decides to overlap the lower boat both on the sides and at the back of the boat. Rosemary's office will be directly over the office I use in the bottom of the hull. Symbolic!

It's like the wooden boat is being moored on top of the metal hull, another river marriage.

The design calls for a door on the river side opening toward the front of the boat. Sam is planning a veranda to run all along that side of the boat, past the suicide windows of the bay and out to the front deck. It's a beautiful solution. I just can't help but wonder how he's going to hang it there.

Welding

The answer is WELDING. He tells me he'll weld braces from the side of the metal boat up to the level of the proposed veranda, then weld horizontal supports for the veranda itself, plus a railing going the entire length of that side of the boat to the front deck. The door from Rosemary's office will open onto the back end of the veranda.

I watch. I'm ready to sort of retire, myself. The problem with being a painter or writer, nobody tells you to stop. You need to recognize, yourself, when you don't want to do it anymore or what you do isn't satisfactory to you, yourself, or any potential readers or lovers of paintings. I don't believe I've reached that point, but I'd probably be the last to know. I do know I don't want to join in this wild welding scheme. I can help with the placing of the veranda planks when the framework is done and do some painting of wood or framework, but that's about it.

Sam says he's already contacted Tom and he's agreed to come out and help build the office and veranda. He estimates it can be done in a month, before it starts being too cold.

I watch the first few days of work, then can't stand it anymore. I bury myself in work down at my desk. I've started another book. It's less strenuous work than painting, and definitely less strenuous than what they'll be doing.

Down there, directly under them, I can hear all the tearing up and hammering as they work. I concentrate on my Macintosh, my recent toy, and thank the powers that be for the money I now have that enables me to pay others to do the kind of work I really don't do very well.

I stop each morning before they arrive on the RER to see what they've done. First, for the office, they build up a platform for the new floor, then put up the studs and rafters for the roof. It's beautiful in the sunlight, the raw wood against the blue autumn sky. Later, they lay the floor and cut out a door from our bedroom into the office. One goes down two steep steps into the bedroom. This is necessary to give enough headroom in the office. Our bedroom has a very low ceiling, just low enough to clear my head.

It is about now that a most interesting encounter takes place. I'm outside repairing our railing along the sides of the gangplank. A couple, younger than us but not young, stops to watch me and keeps smiling. I walk over to see if I can help.

"You don't remember us, do you?"

This is a truly petite blond woman with glinting eyes. She's speaking a blend of American and English English.

"Should I? You do look vaguely familiar. From where would I know you?"

"From death itself."

This is said by the man, a very thin, tall, almost cadaverous man with a somewhat smug smile. He stares into my eyes. They both start laughing.

I'm baffled. Then they start telling me some of the things I've already written into this book. These are the people who, over twenty years ago, when I was pulling all the things out of the boat and almost died from the sulfuric acid, saved my life by dragging me, practically lifeless, down to their boat, where they and their kids nursed me back to life.

We shake hands all around and they recount what happened

those days when I was half-conscious. It turns out she's a writer, too. She's from Chicago, but has lived with her Canadian husband in Winnipeg all these years. He's an engineer and works at the university in Winnipeg. They have five children and come to France once a year as a part of Don's job. Don is his name, Carol is hers. She publishes under her married name, Carol Shields, and recently won the Pulitzer Prize for fiction with her book *Stone Diaries*.

Now, I've read all of her books and they might well be some of the best books I've read in the last ten years. She writes very intimately with great strength. There's a quality of whimsy and a sort of quilt-making mentality putting together little pieces carefully, convoluted and controlled. She also writes beautiful poetry and was first published as a poet. I don't believe in coincidence anymore. We've since become fast friends and see each other every time they come to France. They've even bought themselves a country home in the Vosges.

Now we get back to this story.

Chapter XIX

Bringing It Together

OUR ENTIRE BOAT is littered with small sets of one, two or three steps as one walks its length. There are also narrow double doors in teak between almost every room. It's great for holding heat in a particular room but maddening to be constantly opening and closing doors in the winter. Coming in the front door, one closes that, then there are a pair of doors into the living room that must be closed also. Immediately after that are two steps. On the other side of the living room is another pair of doors to be opened and closed, with a step down before coming to the bathroom door, which also must be opened and closed. There are two steps up to the john. Then, only the toilet seat needs closing.

When one comes out of the john, in order to enter our bedroom there are three steps up and another pair of doors.

Now we have another door and two more steps down into Rosemary's office. It's a bizarre way to have things arranged, but it seems to work. Each room has its own level, its own privacy. Of course I'm not even going again into the stair situation to the bottom of the boat, or the doors between rooms down there.

When it's finished, Rosemary's office is beautiful. They've lined the walls with wood, and bookshelves are installed around two sides. It's floored in a tan nubbed rug and the entire effect is very much like Rosemary, subdued and gracious but not slickly elegant. I promise her a new Macintosh PowerBook to celebrate her retirement. With this, she can really keep up with her massive correspondence, write the book she's been threatening since I've known her and organize a database on all her kindergarten children. Everything she really ought to know about her kindergartners, she'll know.

Her door by her desk is another suicide jump. It steps right out into the river. The project will be to build the veranda. I keep calling it a porch, but Rosemary insists on veranda. After all, it's being built for her.

It soon becomes apparent that two people are not going to be enough to do the welding of the veranda onto the boat. Sam has it all worked out, but he winds up standing in our small rocking dinghy with the power box, oxygen bottles and a quiver full of welding sticks. Tom is leaning over, handing him parts as he needs them, but somebody needs to hold the support bars in place and *still,* while Sam gets a flux started and can make a good weld to the side of the boat. I also wind up with the job of cleaning off the paint and rust from the sides of the boat where Sam intends to weld. Sometimes, I'm leaning out one of those dining room French doors, my feet tied to a support post so I won't go head over heels into the water. Or sometimes I'm in the boat with Sam. Either way, it's not very comfortable. To be honest, my arms feel as if they're being pulled out of their sockets. I'm definitely getting too old for this kind of thing.

To make it worse, the moron who runs the boat club keeps roaring up and down the river beside the sculls in a motorboat with a megaphone. He's shouting something totally incomprehensible to me into his megaphone at the scullers, but, most of all, he's making waves. There's no way one can spot-weld while standing in a boat going up and down. We keep hollering at him, but he can't hear anything over the sound of his motorboat and his own loud shouting at the scullers. Sometimes, because of the bouncing, it takes as many as five sticks just to make one weld. But it gets done. The supports are then welded to a long piece across the top, some more fun, but they hold.

Sam now has a way to stand up out over the space where the veranda will be. He welds more support pieces horizontally from this top horizontal to the diagonal supports going down to the boat. The next part is relatively easy. This is building the rail along the outside of the veranda-porch.

The Finishing Touches

We go down the next weekend and buy oak from the lumbermill near our mill. Sam has all the measurements, and we cut the oak down there with his power saw. We could never bring up all this heavy two-centimeter-thick oak. It's in three-meter lengths when we buy it.

We have, by this time, bought another station wagon, a VW Passat. It isn't new but it's one of the newest cars I've had in a long time, twelve years old. It's perfect for going out on painting trips or hauling anything. We also have, for Rosemary, a ten-year-old Mercedes 200 in perfect shape. We bought both cars from people who were going back to America after serving their stint for their companies here in Paris.

Ah, the glories of extra money, but not too much. The poor old Hillman Husky finally gives up the ghost. We asked too much of it. The Simca begins being too hard and expensive to maintain. It's also always stopping in the most inconvenient places, like in the middle of the Place de la Concorde. With some money, we are less willing to suffer the inconveniences of these cars.

Driving up to Paris in the VW Passat with a load of at least two hundred kilograms of wood for the veranda, a drive of three hundred kilometers, mostly on autoroutes, is some scene. It challenges in "nervous making" almost any of the trips I'd made around Port Marly building the boat. But, again, we make it. Maybe as I grow older, I'm just made nervous more easily.

Matt and I paint the wood before we slip it into place on the veranda. We use one of those paints that not only makes the wood look good (dark oak again) but protects it from all the little beasties that like to eat wood. We have all the boards numbered as to how they fit in, because the veranda varies in size from one meter to almost two. They fit in without any trouble, and then we can have the fun of walking out any of those doors past the bay along one side to the upper deck or back to Rosemary's office. We hang flower boxes along the railing. I paint the railing black, and we plant geranium in long pots with wells under them to hold water.

We paint the hull sort of geranium colors. It's two shades of green, a light green of a geranium leaf with sun shining through it and a darker green of the top of a leaf on a clear day reflecting blue sky. We also have pots of geranium all along the sides of the front deck. We buy a lawn table with six chairs and put them at a wide space near Rosemary's office window.

On the other side of the table and chairs is the window opening over the kitchen sink. This makes it so we can pass food out from the kitchen directly to where we eat. I build a folding platform to make this easy. We begin eating breakfast, lunch and dinner out there whenever the weather is good, or even just good enough.

Obviously we've moved permanently into the boat. We begin to realize this is the last of our nests. This is where we'll retire. We hope to travel, because this is one of Rosemary's dreams, but the boat will be home.

We've discovered the joy of taking a little rowboat out and rowing slowly upriver on a late sunny evening and drifting back with the flow of the river. Sometimes we fish from the veranda. The water is cleaner and lighter every day. The only time we smell the river-sewer smell is when we have the boat closed up for several weeks and only when we come in. After we open the windows, it's cleared out in ten minutes.

The village of Port Marly is developing the *chemin de halage*, a bit at a time, into a most lovely pathway with a park along its length, with slides, seesaws and sandboxes for little children. The intention is to call it *La Promenade des Impressionnistes.*

To encourage the idea, I regularly put paintings in the windows on the land side of the boat so strollers can see some paintings even if they aren't by Impressionists. Once in a while I put paintings on the water side, for the scullers.

We have eleven different restaurants of all kinds in our town, from the two *restaurants de routiers,* to fancy French restaurants, one with specialties of Savoie—cheese fondue and raclette—another with an American ambiance called Buffalo Grill. There are also specialty restaurants, Chinese, Vietnamese, Italian, Mexican. They're all quite good. We can eat better here, and for less, than in Paris. There is a barbershop, two bakeries, several antique stores, a drugstore, a small grocery and, of course, the café of Alfred Sisley. Port Marly, along the Seine, is a regular small French village.

We're well known in the village now, and more or less accepted. There are more boats, and some of the people on them are quite interesting, a good *mélange* of nationalities, with boat ownership a common denominator.

Across the street from us is a doctor's office with two young women general practitioners, each with young children. They are quite efficient and give us very good frontline medical care under the auspices of French Social Security. When there is need for more complex or elaborate medical analysis, they refer us to *La Clinique de l'Europe,* a modern hospital, just a five-minute walk up the hill behind them. I often go to the doctor or the hospital in my slippers. It's all extremely low key and high quality.

For a long time, M. Teurnier would wave, or sometimes stop, when he was going up or down the river to help some other poor soul whose boat is in trouble. Once I invite him aboard, and while we're chatting I do an oil sketch of a portrait, not bad for me. (I'm not a very good portraitist.) But he likes it and I give it to him. He doesn't seem to change, although he must be over eighty now.

People who visit often ask if there's any chance they could buy a boat, and do I think they'd enjoy it. It's a hard question to answer. It's one of the reasons I wrote this book. If someone thinks they can live through the kind of misery we did and stick it out, or has natural skills like Sam's, I say go to it. Living on a boat is not easy, but it's fun, a never-ending challenge that can lend a real uniqueness to life.

CHAPTER XX

Blood in the Street

ALTHOUGH LIVING ON a houseboat is very pleasant, what with being on the water and separated from the shore by the length of a gangplank, life has had its interesting, often amusing, sometimes frightening, moments.

Also, Port Marly itself is generally a quiet village, set aside from most of the surrounding bedroom communities by the N13 highway on the one side and the Seine on the other. However there have been some moments of high drama over the past twenty or so years we've been living on the river.

We've been here over twenty years, have our boat tightly moored to the *berge,* are well accepted in the community, and are gradually beginning what turns out to be a lifetime activity of maintenance. A houseboat, like a yacht, maybe even more so, takes continual care. One can even say, as with a yacht, that's it's a hole in the water into which one shovels or throws money.

One day, I'm up on the roof trying to repair holes that have been poked through during the last river rage. This time, we went up four and a half meters. I'm unrolling tar paper when I hear some horn blowing, a scream, then a shout from up on the road. I can see from high on the boat roof that two cars are parked in the street at the intersection where Rue de Paris meets Rue Jean-Jaurès. I think there might have been a traffic accident, so I quickly climb down from the roof and run through the public garden up toward the café on the corner to see if I can help.

When I arrive there, Pierre, the man who runs the restaurant just across the Rue de Paris from where we normally park our car, is standing outside his car with the door open.

His son, Sebastian, is on the curb. Behind Pierre's auto is a second auto. The driver of this car is also standing in the street. The two of them are screaming and shouting at each other. I look, but there's no glass on the street and no other sign of an accident. Just then, as I arrive, the man in the second car dashes toward Pierre and takes a good roundhouse swing at him. This surprises me, because most French attack with their feet. Also, it's obvious this man does not know Pierre is a black-belt judo instructor. But he finds out in a hurry.

Faster than the eye, at least my eye, by some Oriental martial magic, the man is on his back in the street. It doesn't seem as if Pierre has moved a muscle. Now, I *am* shocked, not so much by the fact that the man is on his back but because he'd actually taken a swing at Pierre. The French law is very clear and strict about these impromptu street encounters. Regardless of fault, in the case of a dispute, the person who touches the other first is wrong. So, perhaps our visitor flat in the street made two mistakes. First, he attacked a black-belt judo expert, and secondly, he broke the French law. Now he looks as if he's broken more than the law.

He slowly pulls himself to his feet, rubbing the back of his hand across his bleeding nose. How the nose got to bleeding I'll never know. I saw everything and I saw nothing.

Suddenly, again so quickly, I hardly see it, the young man reaches into his pocket, pulls out a knife and drives it into the stomach of Pierre! Pierre stands there looking down at the place where the knife has, so silently, been driven in and pulled out again. What kind of judo is this? Blood is already spurting from the wound. Pierre's pulling up his sweater and shirt to see what's happened. His boy, Sebastian, is still standing there on the curb beside me, not seeming to know what's happened any more than I do.

The man is already in his auto, twisting it sharply. He drives past and away down the street. Stupidly, I don't think to take down the license-plate number. Luckily, Mme. Colombe, who lives in an apartment just over the doctor's office, is not so stupid. She also runs down and tells Dr. Avignat what has happened.

Sebastian and I are on the road beside Pierre, who has dropped to his knees. I'm not usually squeamish about blood, but this is an exceptional amount of blood. Obviously an important artery had been severed. I stretch Pierre out on the street and try to stanch the blood by holding my hand over the wound. I'm getting nowhere. People have started running out from the café. It's one of those times I really wish I could speak adequate French. Everyone is leaning over, just watching, as if we're giving some kind of Red Cross CPR lesson. Poor Sebastian has been crying, but now he's passed out. He's a very sensitive and sensible boy. Pierre is completely white and barely conscious.

Dr. Avignat drops beside me in the street. She has her black bag and pulls a large compress out of it. She takes my hand and moves it from over the wound up toward Pierre's heart. She shouts something to the bystanders. One turns and goes back to the café. She gives the number of the clinic up the hill. She's wrapped a large compress all around Pierre's stomach and jammed several large gauze compresses under it, but the blood keeps seeping out. I look at her. Her face is white, too. How do doctors do it?

I hear the ambulance coming down the hill. It's not more than five minutes after she'd asked someone to call. Perhaps the same smart woman, Mme. Colombe, who took down the license-plate number and called the doctor, also called SAMU, the emergency help number. When the ambulance arrives, two white-coated men jump out and, at a sign from the doctor, attach a bottle of what looks like plasma to Pierre's arm. Dr. Avignat also gives him an injection in the other arm. She has out her blood-pressure cuff, wraps it onto Pierre's arm and pumps. She's also checking Pierre's pulse. She looks into Pierre's eyes by lifting his closed lid. She's shaking her head. I can't believe it either.

We slide the stretcher under Pierre and the doctor climbs into the ambulance with the others. The horn is beeping the French emergency "hee-haw" sound, and the blue lights are flashing. In a minute, the ambulance doors are closed and they're gone. I look over, and Sebastian is sitting up. Mme. Colombe, who lives in the same apartment building where Pierre and his wife live, is talking to him softly. It's only then I realize it's probably she who called the doctor and the ambulance. I help her get Sebastian across the street and into the family restaurant. In the kitchen we find his mother. She'd been so busy she hadn't heard all the excitement.

I ease Sebastian into one of the chairs. He's very pale and crying. Nicole, Pierre's wife, is worried about Sebastian; he looks ghastly. Mme. Colombe is trying to explain what has happened.

Then, Nicole almost faints. For a minute she runs in erratic circles, first burying her hands in her apron, then untying and taking the apron off. Now Sebastian is worried about his mother. I tell Mme. Colombe that I'm going for my auto and I'll drive them up to the hospital. It looks as though each of them will be needing some medical care, as well as information about the condition of Pierre.

As we go by the corner, Pierre's car is still there. Mme. Colombe is trying to explain to Nicole what's happened. There's blood all over the street. Somebody has taken sawdust from somewhere and spread it over the blood so it looks like a spontaneous street butcher shop. I try to drive carefully, but quickly, up the hill to the hospital. I'm awfully shaken myself.

I leave them off at the emergency room door and go park the car. My family should be home in about an hour. I park and dash into the emergency room. They stop me at the desk; my French has completely abandoned me. Mme. Colombe, in the waiting room with Sebastian, calls out and they let me in. Sebastian is crying again. His mother isn't there. He's trying to explain to Mme. Colombe what's happened as he saw it. He keeps asking me if it isn't true. *C'est vrais, monsieur, n'est-ce pas?* I nod, but he's observed more than I did.

He tells how he was walking along the street when he saw his father in their stopped car, waving for him to come over. He'd just started across the street when the automobile behind his father started honking his horn and yelling out the window of his car. Sebastian dashed across the street. At the same time, his father climbed out of his car and moved toward the car behind him. The man back there jumped out, and the two of them started shouting at each other, the man in the other car shaking his fist at Pierre. From there, it was as I saw it. Madame Colombe tells how she got the license number and called the police.

When we'd waited two hours for some word about how things were going in the operation room, I feel I should go home and tell the family where I am. I promise to come back. It all seems so crazy, so sudden, I still can't put it together.

My family's at the boat. I explain what's happened. None of them can understand any more than I can. I tell them I'd promised to come back to the waiting room of the hospital. Rosemary gives me a kiss.

"I'll hold dinner until you can come back, dear. Tell Nicole and Sebastian how sorry we all are."

Up at the hospital, Nicole and Dr. Avignat are sitting with Sebastian and Mme. Colombe. Dr. Avignat is explaining carefully the medical situation. She says Pierre will be all right but he'll need to be in the hospital for some time. He's lost much blood, but the artery has been repaired.

"Only a strong person, such as he, could have survived the loss of so much blood."

She turns to me.

"Did you see what happened? How did this come about?"

I try to tell what I'd seen. She keeps shaking her head.

"I must go back to my practice and see my patients. Could you drive me down, please, M. Wharton?"

I volunteer and Nicole says she'll call a friend to come for her and Sebastian. She thanks me. We leave the hospital and I drive Dr. Avignat to her office.

"M. Wharton, I did not think he could live, but he has a remarkable constitution. We must help the police find this man who did this. He is obviously insane."

Well, it turns out they do catch the man two days later. He is a psychiatric patient who escaped and stole a car. Pierre is home after three weeks in the hospital. He's lost much weight, but seems in good form.

"For three years I've been trying to lose those five kilos, M. Wharton, and now I've lost it in three weeks."

"Yes, Pierre, but mostly in blood."

So, this, for me, was the end of it. Pierre quickly puts back on his five kilos. It is difficult to lose weight when you run a quality restaurant such as his. We remain good friends, in fact, he's the one who arranges a garage for us where we can keep our auto in the winter.

Dog Genius

Another exciting event, but not quite so bloody or traumatic, is the case of the floating pups.

One morning, I look out the window from my desk in the hull

and see a burlap bag floating past. Something inside is wiggling and whining.

I assume someone has thrown in a sack of puppies or kittens to drown them. I dash up on deck. I grab my grappling hook and try retrieving the sack, but can't reach it. I climb down my ladder and into my small dinghy. I'm just pushing off when I see Mr. Cox, the Englishman who sent me the letter about my boat being *coulé*. He's already cast off and fished them into his small skiff. We wave to each other. He rows back to his boat. I know he and his wife are great animal lovers. I tie up my dinghy and walk down the *chemin de halage* to his large barge.

He and his wife have already gotten the sack untied and found five puppies, not more than a few days old, in there. Two of them are already drowned. Mr. Cox is enraged. His wife is in tears.

"Ah, M. Wharton, it is events like this which makes one lose faith in humans. How can anyone know what these small living creatures might have become? They might well have been the beginnings of a new race of genius dogs."

He pauses. His wife has hurried down into their galley and comes up with quickly warmed milk. She even has a small baby bottle into which she's hastily pouring the milk. I suspect this is not the first batch of abandoned animals they've rescued.

"Yes, M. Wharton. There could well have been the Albert Einstein of the dog world in that sack. What a waste."

I point out that there were three of them.

"They couldn't all have been Albert Einstein, Mr. Cox, now, could they."

I'm getting into the spirit of things, all the way to an English accent. He looks at me with a glint in his eye.

"I shall name them. This one with the white spot on its head is Einstein, the one with the white on its paw is Zweistein, and this one with the white on the tip of its tail is Dreistein."

———

The three puppies grow up into huge, more or less black, some-what Labradorish, brutish, vicious hounds. Mr. Cox tries to give me one, but I'm not a dog person. In the course of my life, some people have called me an S.O.B., but I'm not a dog. Also I have a strong aversion to keeping fellow creatures as pets, especially after my canaries. It isn't good for the kept animals or the people who keep them.

Mr. Cox, who is most persuasive, manages to talk two other boat families into taking two of the dogs. He keeps Einstein for himself. The Palstras, an Australian couple farther downriver, take one, the Toys, a Dutch couple, their next-boat neighbors, the other. None of the French boat people are interested. The Le Clercs have recently purchased a gigantic Great Dane, and so are more or less overwhelmed with dog. The Palstras name their dog Simba, appropriate.

Those three sibling dogs grow into a pack. Neither Mr. Cox, nor the Palstras nor the Toys, are great animal keepers, so these ani-mals mostly range freely. That's all right with me, but they *hunt* as a pack, and often their quarry is me. Whether I'm walking, jogging or riding my bike along the *chemin de halage*, they're after me, nipping, snarling, biting, hackles up, making charges, and in gen-eral not living according to the heritage Mr. Cox has bestowed upon them.

I speak to each of the owners about it, but receive thrown-up hands and the usual insistence of most dog owners that their dogs don't bite and I have nothing to worry about. But I'm worried.

One day, after a harried skirmish through a gauntlet of about two hundred yards, I've had it. I buy a small water pistol and fill it with water along with fine red pepper, actually paprika. The next morning when I'm taking my usual bicycle ride, they're waiting. I'm prepared. I bike along slowly; the animals have dispersed in their usual attack positions to surround me. I squirt left and right, aiming for the whites of their eyes. At first there's only surprise, then confusion, then absolute mayhem, as they start rubbing their eyes with their paws, yelping and running in circles. I continue my bicycle ride in peace.

When I return, they're out there waiting for me. I glide slowly into the midst of them. I'm becoming concerned that there isn't one functioning brain cell in the pack, despite Mr. Cox's claims, and they won't learn, but as soon as I pull out my trusty squirt gun, they retreat, barking. I squirt the ones I can reach as additional negative reinforcement. I don't want to carry a squirt pistol the rest of my life, running shotgun on myself.

I do the same routine while pursuing each of my usual modes of locomotion: walking, running, jogging, biking. By the last trial, they're ducking and "ky-yi-yi-ing" back to their respective boats as soon as they see me. Success. I visit with each of the owners and explain what I've done. There's no resistance except from Mr. Cox.

"But that's cruel, Mr. Wharton. They're only dumb animals doing what comes natural to them."

"It's you who insisted they weren't dumb, Mr. Cox; I won't debate that. But I'm an animal only doing what is natural, too, protecting myself from wild animal packs with which I come in contact. Surely, I have the same rights to act naturally as dogs do."

He turns his back to me. I can live with that. After all, I'm still concerned about why an Englishman would send an emergency telegram to an American in French. That doesn't seem very smart. Nice, yes; smart, no. I think Herr Einstein himself would agree with that.

Unwilling Baptism

We have a young French couple two boats upriver, toward Paris, on the other side of the pirate boat. They are recently married and have a lovely little boy. They are very Catholic and conservative.

They are members of a church in Port Marly that has a reputation throughout France. The church is in pure Jesuit style architecture, but that isn't the reason for its fame. It is the only church in France where the Mass is still conducted in Latin.

This is because the pastor of this church is a very good and old friend of the archbishop. The archbishop, an elderly, conservative man, has been given some kind of special dispensation to continue the Latin Mass despite Vatican rules. French people for many miles around come especially to this church on Sundays for the ten o'clock Latin Mass. These are some of the most conservative people in the country, both religiously and politically. Our neighbors, who seem so much like the ordinary French young, are part of this French Catholic subgroup that is primarily made up of older people—people for whom the only real Mass is said in Latin.

The old archbishop dies. When the new archbishop is installed, he cancels the dispensation and insists that the Mass in this church now be said in French. The priest bows to the desires of his scattered parish, not the archbishop, nor the Vatican, and continues saying the Latin Mass.

I don't know all the details of the confrontation, but somehow, there comes a Sunday when, during the Latin Mass, the CRS, a paramilitary police group much used by the French authorities for crowd and mob control, charges into the church and pulls the pastor off the altar in mid-Mass. When the communicants, the participants at the Mass, start to object by throwing chairs around, the CRS begins bopping parishioners on the head and throwing them into the Black (now blue) Marias outside. It's quite a scene.

After that, for many months, one side or the other would barricade the church from the other, sitting vigils through the night to see the wrong Masses won't be said, wrong depending on which side you back. Young François, since he lives so close to the church, stands many of these guard duties, protecting his church against the godless who want the Mass in French. I suggest to him one time that one Mass could be in French, the other in Latin, but he only frowns at my simplicity as if I were an infidel. Which I probably am, by his standards.

This is only to show what a good family man François is.

One late spring morning, I think it was a Saturday, I'm on the bank beside my boat, pulling up nettles. These nettles start growing in spring, and even though I pull them out by the roots, they come up every year. They can take over the entire bank and grow to more than four feet high. Because they really sting, I'm wearing gloves, hanging on to the bank and pulling them out from the bottom so as to get the roots, one more time.

I look up and, dashing past me on the *chemin de halage,* is François, running like mad and pulling off his clothes and tossing them as he goes! He runs past me, then up our gangplank onto our front deck. I run with him, figuring maybe this is some extension of the church battle up the street and they're about ready to take over our boat to hold services. I want to tell him it's the boat next door, the Le Clercs' boat, that's the one they once fitted out as a church for the river people.

When I reach him, he's hopping up and down, pulling off his shoes, staring out into the water. Now I hear the screaming from his boat. Also in the water, swimming toward us, is another man. He's swimming downstream like crazy. I'm completely confused. At this moment, François climbs to the edge of my deck and throws himself into the water. I look down and he's swimming furiously out toward the center of the river. Then I see it, rising briefly from the water, a small body.

François sees it too, and moves forward with a burst of speed. He goes under for what seems forever, then comes up, pulling what I can see is a small child behind him.

I've come out of my trance and I'm down the ladder and into my dinghy. I row toward them as they drift downriver. I yell out to

François and bear onto the oars. I position the boat downriver and François hands the baby up to me. He's coughing out water and crying. François tries to pull himself into the boat, but is too weak and waterlogged. His friend, who was also swimming in this race against death, has worked his way over to the bank and pulled himself out in dripping wet clothes, shoes and all. I put the baby into the bottom of the dinghy and pull François in. He struggles and falls to his knees in the dinghy with the baby between his legs. He starts pumping on the baby's chest. I row toward shore.

When we get there, a crowd is waiting. Someone has gone for Dr. Avignat, someone else takes the baby and starts artificial respiration. It's François's little boy. I haven't done anything, but I'm pooped. I tie up my dinghy and climb onto the *chemin de halage* with everyone. I hear the baby cry. François's wife is holding the baby now over her knees and patting him on the back; she's white and close to fainting. Dr. Avignat is checking everything and smiling. All's well that ends well.

Alicia, François's wife, will not live on the boat again. She goes to a hotel in town. François moves their things out and sells the houseboat. The baby is fine. A year later, Alicia has another baby, a little girl. They keep in contact with their friends on the boats, but Alicia never goes on one again. François, for two years, helps keep the faith with the church, standing guard. The archbishop has the church closed down completely as a place of worship until things calm down, if they ever will.

Chapter XXI

Impatience

NEITHER MY WIFE nor I are great gardeners, but like most people, we enjoy flowers and shrubs. We both have a weakness for roses. Early on, we buy six roses and plant them just inside the fence, next to the end of the gangplank. The first year they do well, so we decide to expand. We drive to a *pépinière*, a place where they sell bushes and flowers. We do go a bit overboard! Maybe that isn't an appropriate description for someone living on a boat!

When we leave, we are the proud owners of a flowering Japanese cherry tree, six more rosebushes, two hundred tulip bulbs, plus an assortment of other bulbs. We have ten flats of impatiens of varying colors and about fifty pounds of grass seed guaranteed to grow in the shade, of which we have much on our bank.

We rake and dig and pull up weeds, mostly *orties* (nettles), until the bank is bare. We pour on ten sacks of fertilizer, somewhat superfluous, considering the rich soil left by the river in the wake of each flood, but we're into doing things properly. Next, we plant our tulips over the bank, along with narcissus, daffodil and crocus. After this, I hand-spread our special shade-oriented grass.

Soon, with much loving care and watering, we possess a gorgeous lawn, a lawn we have no intention of mowing. The bank is too steep. There are tulips growing like brightly colored Easter eggs over the *berge*. We also have the springlike sprouting of other bulbs, a scattering of yellow, white and purple. The whole thing looks like an Easter basket. We know the garden is very amateurish, but we love it.

One Sunday, I look out the window and there are fishermen scattered, like dragons, throughout our Easter basket. They are tramping down our new grass, our tulips, our carefully planted impatiens. Speak of impatience! I run out onto the gangplank shouting and screaming at them as if I'm a madman. I am mad, not crazy-mad, but very "angry-mad." They shout back how the bank is public property and they can use it if they want, but, finally, reluctantly leave. Most of them are teenagers.

It is apparent that both for our convenience and the safety of others, as well as the survival of our garden, we must build a fence along the top of our *berge* at the edge of the *chemin de halage*. The Le Clercs have a fence all around their property, except on the river edge. It's about five feet high, made of sharpened pickets placed close together. It makes their *berge* virtually a fortress. This is reinforced by a heavy oaken door with a large bell that must be rung before the door will be opened. It allows for a maximum of privacy, and many days I envy them, but it's illegal. I don't know how they got away with it. One cannot erect a fence along the *chemin de halage* that cannot be seen through and is higher than a man can step over. I know my inseam is thirty inches, so I decide to build a pointed picket fence thirty-two inches high, the length of Matt's inseam. It seems fair enough, a compromise.

I paint it dark brown, the color of the earth along the bank, so it won't violate the visual purity of things. It works out very well, so much so that several other boat people erect similar fences at low cost, since the pickets are only roof lathing and the cut I've designed doesn't call for much wastage. I also buy a sign saying ATTENTION CHIEN MÉCHANT!!! That is, Look out, mean dog. I put this sign on the door to the gangplank.

It seems to help, at least we don't have fishermen in our garden. Feeling guilty, I build a small wooden dock between our *berge* and our upriver neighbor, just for the fishermen. That's OK except that fishermen in general are loud, and worse yet, *early*!

But live and let live. However, the next season, I buy ten pyracantha bushes and plant them all along the fence. They have a lovely year-round green leaf, are fast growing, and produce beautiful, small, highly fragrant blossoms, then gorgeous red, yellow and orange berries. Most important, they are covered with stiff, sharp thorns! We are rapidly becoming more than amateur as gardeners.

Per Square Meter

When we first bought the boat, our fee for the right to park it on the river, called our *droit de stationnement,* was paid to the local city hall of Le Port Mairie. It was the grand sum of sixty-nine francs a year, or about fifteen dollars. We had a legitimate *droit de stationnement* because of the Arctic explorer who put the boat in place originally. This declared *droit de stationnement* became important in determining *our* right to stay. As time passes, the cost of this "right" goes up a bit at a time, nothing serious. Then, *Les Ponts et Chaussées* at Bougival contact us and want some money paid to the state of France for the space we take up in the river, as well as the place along the *berge.* We agree. The figure they quote per year is not outrageous.

Then, there's the question as to whether the boat in the water now is indeed the boat to which the *droit de stationnement* had been granted. The original wooden boat was named *Le bateau Lymnée,* named after a small mammal in the Arctic. The point they're making is that this boat is no longer in the water, and the metal hull we have now is merely a beheaded corpse to a boat that is functioning on the river as a pusher. In other words, the cabin and the motor constitute the real boat, not the crew cabin and oil cargo section we had bought.

This discussion goes on for over three years, during which we cannot be sure our boat is legitimately moored. It brings about many a sleepless night for me, the great worrier. This all comes up well after the incredible effort with Sam to secure the boat safely.

Finally, in desperation, I send Rosemary, my kindergarten-teacher wife, to discuss the problem with M. Le Cerb at *Les Ponts et Chaussées* in Bougival, three kilometers upriver. After all her years of taming kindergarten children, a mere director for the rivers and bridges of France is as nothing. It's decided, albeit begrudgingly, that they will accord to our beloved monstrosity the rights and privileges originally pertaining to the *Bateau Lymnée,* but we cannot use the name of the barge, *Ste. Marie-Thérèse,* as the boat name for postal references. Ste. Marie-Thérèse is the name painted on the bow of our metal hull. I paint it over.

The final round is working out the system whereby the value of mooring places will be established by *Les Ponts et Chaussées.* It's decided to charge by the square meters of displaced water in the river. For this, our boat, at twenty-seven meters by five meters, comes to one hundred and thirty-five square meters, for which we are to pay twenty francs per square meter per year, the sum of twenty-seven hundred francs. That, too, we think is fair enough, but many of our neighbors can't, or won't pay, and organize a group of riverboat inhabitants to fight the decisions made. In the end, I hope "in the end," it is agreed to accept the decisions regarding the square-meter proposal, the cost per meter being equivalent, approximately, to cost per square meter of land for rent on the banks of the river, although none of the land on the river is rented. It's a complicated but interesting conclusion, very French. We, in our family, are mostly interested in maintaining our mooring at almost any cost. We now have such a commitment, both economically and emotionally, to the river life we're living. We dread giving it up.

The Swimming Rabbit

As a kindergarten teacher, Rosemary had kept, despite my qualms about captive animals, quite a menagerie of small pets. There is at a minimum, one rabbit, usually dwarf, several guinea pigs, some hamsters that are always escaping, a turtle and goldfish. In spring there is also a contingent of three baby ducklings. By June, these are no longer ducklings, but full-grown, quacking monsters. By that time, the children in kindergarten are afraid of them. Usually, it's Memorial Day, May Day in France, when we take the ducks down to our old water mill in Burgundy and put them on the pond, where they live happy lives.

Most short vacations, such as Christmas or Easter, Rosemary can work it out with some of the parents to take one or more of our zoo home with them. But the long summer holiday is another affair. "Farming out" our farm to an American community that is mostly transient can be a challenge. Often, we take a good part of the beasts down to the mill, including the turtle and goldfish. When our children were young, these pets were always well cared for and gave much pleasure.

But one Easter, we can't find a place for the rabbit. This is a surprise and something of a shock, because usually at Easter the rabbit is easily placed. We aren't going to take Jimmy, the rabbit, down with us; it's too difficult to transport him except in a cage, and we don't have enough space in the auto. We decide to leave him in my studio with an adequate supply of proper rabbit food and some water. Even the children, after much consideration, are convinced Jimmy will be all right.

After Easter, we aren't back at the boat five minutes, having had a fine relaxing holiday in the beautiful countryside, when Mme. Le Clerc is at our door. She's holding Jimmy by the ears in her arms. She asks if the rabbit is ours. My first impulse is to deny. I don't know how she's gotten the rabbit, and I don't want to know. From Mme. Le Clerc's face, I can tell it's trouble.

"M. Wharton, I know this must have something to do with you and your family."

I invite her into the boat. She keeps a firm hold on Jimmy's ears. She stares at me, madly, in the eyes.

"I was looking out from my kitchen window in my dressing gown and what do you think I saw?"

I figure a wild guess won't hurt.

"A rabbit?"

"Yes. It was a white rabbit swimming past our boat. A white rabbit all smeared with black oil. You know, monsieur, rabbits are not supposed to swim."

"Yes, I know that."

"I called for Claude to launch the small boat and catch this phenomenon, this white rabbit swimming down the river on Easter morning."

I wait. This is even worse than I expected. I'm wondering how Jimmy escaped. It doesn't seem possible. Maybe he chewed his way through the metal hull and the boat is in the process of sinking.

"Claude made a heroic rescue just as this rabbit was about to drown. He brought him back to our boat and his fur was all stuck down with water and oil. It was a very sad-looking rabbit. Is it really yours, M. Wharton?"

Here's another chance to deny, get out of it, like Saint Peter, but she'd never believe me, anyway.

"No, Mme. Le Clerc, it is my wife's."

Rosemary has come over at the critical moment to soothe shattered nerves. She reaches out for Jimmy, lifts him by his ears from Mme. Le Clerc's grasp and cuddles him in her arms.

"Yes, it is the rabbit of my kindergarten. The children will be so pleased you saved him. Thank you."

Mme. Le Clerc isn't willing to let go as easily as that.

"It took all the afternoon to clean and dry the poor creature and to feed it. It was starving. It really is a very nice rabbit; we've become quite attached to it. Are you sure you would like to keep it?"

Rosemary gives her a very professional smile and pets the rabbit once more.

"Oh, yes. We must have it. The children would be so unhappy if I did not bring him back tomorrow when school starts. I shall tell them of Jimmy's adventure and about how you and M. Le Clerc so heroically saved him. Is it possible for you to come to our school with me so they can meet you? It would be very exciting for them. Perhaps M. Le Clerc can come, too."

I figure she's gone too far. Rosemary can set up the most incredible scenes without trying. She should be in the U.N. She's wasted on kindergarten children. Mme. Le Clerc breaks all out in smiles.

"I would like to, and so would Claude, but we can't. I don't speak English, and the children are all American in your class, aren't they? Thank you so much for inviting us."

"That's unfortunate, Mme. Le Clerc. But I assure you, when I tell them the story of the escape and rescue, they will want to write thank-you notes to you and your husband."

She's done it again. Mme. Le Clerc leaves smiling. I take Jimmy downstairs and put him into his cage, feed him, although there was plenty of food left, and look for how he could have gotten out. There's, of course, no hole in the hull but, by searching around, I find where he'd climbed up the staircase ladder and squeezed between the two boats and thence onto the deck, from which he probably took a plunge, purposefully or accidentally, I'll never know, into the Seine. So be it.

That next day, Rosemary, after carrying off Jimmy in the car to school, tells, with great dramatics, I'm sure, the story of Jimmy's adventure in the Seine to the kindergarten children. Then she puts out paper, pencils and crayons so they can draw and write thank-you notes. There are wonderful pictures of M. Le Clerc pulling Jimmy out of the Seine, of Mme. Le Clerc looking out her window in her dressing gown at Jimmy floating down the river, of M. and Mme. Le Clerc cleaning and feeding Jimmy.

That evening, Rosemary delivers all the notes along with a bouquet of flowers one of the mothers has brought to her as teacher. M. and Mme. Le Clerc are delighted. So ends the drama. Thus, despite a bad beginning moving the boat into place, we have good relations with our downriver neighbors.

Our Garage

Although Port Marly, along the banks of the Seine, is a small town, it has most of the services one would find in any French village. Along with our ten restaurants, we have several garages servicing and selling autos, from Volkswagens through Alfa Romeos to Mercedes. There is one small garage at the end of the Rue de Paris that specializes in repairing American autos.

We have our repairs done there, although we don't have any American autos, because the place was so highly recommended, and also because we've consistently had good work done there on our antiquated autos.

Another reason is that André, the chief mechanic, is such a special person. He looks like a university professor and is very willing to explain any work that needs to be done on our long-suffering autos. He also gently explains what the alternatives are to the repairs he suggests. He is very good about letting me stay around the shop and watch the work in progress. I keep hoping someday I'll be able to fix my own autos, but as I progress in what I know about the insides of automobiles, they in turn become more and more complicated, so I've lost hope.

André is also willing for me to paint in the shop, the atelier. During minor operations on our motorized fleet, I've made some of my best paintings, right there on the shop floor. Every time I see him, he asks how my painting is coming along, and sometimes comes up to our boat to see the work. I gave him several photocopies of the paintings I've done, along with an original sketch of him leaning into the maw of a huge Cadillac; not ours, thank God.

The owner of the shop walks his dog past our boat every day along the *chemin de halage* and stops to look at the paintings I keep changing in the windows of the boat. He's always asking when I'll be showing in Paris. I read somewhere that everybody should have a good mechanic and a good dentist. I add to that a good doctor. We have all, except the dentist, here in Port Marly.

The Laundry

We originally had an American washer and dryer on the front deck of the boat. We'd bought them from Americans at the American School of Paris who were going back to the States. They lasted three years, but then the continual damage from the weather destroyed the washer and damaged the dryer. In time, I threw out the washer and moved the dryer inside into the front cabin, where it still is, despite a few replacements of the drive belt and a solenoid.

So, now, on the way to do our shopping in Le Pecq at the Casino market, we drive to the local Laundromat and do the wash. After the shopping, we stop by and pick up the wet clothes, which we then take home and put in the dryer. It works out quite well.

There is also, near us, an old woman who takes in wash and irons it by hand. It's grimly expensive and we can't afford it, but I love to watch her. She doesn't use an electric iron but has an old cast iron one sitting on a stove to keep it hot, and she continually checks it to maintain just the right temperature.

It's like watching a ballet to see her iron a shirt with that iron, all the right movements and never a moment's hesitation or delay.

Twice I've painted her, once from the window and once from the deep corner of her tiny workroom, looking out past her and through the window into the street. While I was painting her, I'd bring a good glass of beer from the *routier* café across the street. Each time, she'd nurse it for about an hour. I did some good paintings and had interesting conversations with this gentle, hardworking old lady. I took photos of the two paintings, had them enlarged and gave them to her. She couldn't believe what I'd done and stuck them on the wall in front of her with shirt pins.

The Barber

Our barbershop, also Rosemary's *coiffeur*, is just up Jean-Jaurès from the boat. M. Dubois is the proprietor. He gives me a very good haircut and trims my beard about once a month. Rosemary goes just about as often. He starts with washing the hair and does mostly scissor-clipping and, if necessary, works with thinning shears. In my case, this isn't necessary; my hair thins itself, somewhat overenthusiastically, but my beard can sometimes use some thinning. Each time I have a haircut, I'm so pleased I wonder why I don't go more often. It doesn't take long to look for the answer. It costs too much.

M. Dubois is one of the best sources of information about what's going on in the town. He's a part of the local administration and shares willingly what he knows as he clips away. His wife has had a bad hip and finally a hip-replacement operation, so she limps. It's been much pain and it shows on her face, although she's a very kind and attractive woman.

Bakers

We have two bakeries. One, quite close on Jean-Jaurès and the other up on the Route de Versailles. The nearer one is more a *pâtisserie,* with fancy cakes, etc., as well as bread. The other has better bread, but nothing fancy. Unfortunately, it's a longer walk up there, so we often use the nearer shop. The owner of the shop on Jean-Jaurès has been in several competitions for fancy foods and has trophies and awards to show for it in the window of his shop. He also does some catering.

The Grocer

There is a grocery store at the corner of Jean-Jaurès and Rue de Paris. This store has had quite a history just in the time we've been on the boat. It was originally run by an older couple who didn't keep up with things, so it came to be a place where you bought only emergency items, things you forgot while shopping. Or sometimes on Monday, when the regular shops were closed, one would shop there.

They sell the shop to a young couple. These young people really work to make the place go. They keep their stock up and prices much different than at the large stores in Paris, Le Pecq, or St.-Germain-en-Laye. They put in a Xerox and a fax machine and are generous with their prices to use them. It comes in handy for me often. They stay on for about five years, then realize it's too small a place and too much work to justify the small profit they make. We all, everyone in the village, hate to see them give up.

They sell to an Algerian family. The whole family works in the store. They pile up stock all over the floor, and nobody seems to know where anything is. Also, the person who works at the cashier never heard of public relations and can't count very well, at least when it comes to the money he is supposed to give in change. Also, the prices often aren't marked, so it's something like a street market, too much negotiation. They've recently hired a young woman, not in the family, who is very good. People who had stopped using the shop are starting to use it again. But I don't really know how long they can survive in such a small place. I hope it goes on because a small grocery like that really is a "convenience store." It's convenient.

When we moved into Port Marly, there was another grocery store down the Rue de Paris. This one was really small and called *Le trou dans le mur,* that is, "the hole in the wall." And it really was just about that. A middle-aged woman ran it by herself. There were items hanging from any wall space and counters packed so densely one could scarcely move around. Her advantages were that she was open when the other stores were closed, such as Sunday afternoons and Mondays. Also she was open as late as ten o'clock in the evening. She didn't open until five, so her whole trade was marginal.

She was a very pleasant woman, and if you could wait, she'd manage to supply almost anything in the line of *alimentation* you might want. She sold Metro tickets and lottery tickets, also cigarettes and matches, all monopolies of the state. She'd buy them en masse and sell them to people who didn't have the time to go through the town to the *tabac* which was the official dispenser of such items. I'd often walk down there, mostly to watch her hustle from five in the afternoon until ten at night. She was a whirlwind, and although the shop was frequently filled with people, one rarely had to wait. She was a blessing for those whose schedules, sleeping or working, were out of sync with the normal diurnal lives most of us lead.

The door into the shop was narrow and low, so one needed to duck. Sometimes I wondered if the store really existed at all, it was like a hobbit place. She was next door to the *routier* restaurant and did a fairly brisk trade with those driving trucks and stopping for an evening meal.

Around ten years ago I went by and the *trou* had been filled in, plastered over. I don't know what happened, but for years her painted sign remained, LE TROU DANS LE MUR. I've often wondered what the casual visitor to our town thought when they saw the sign and found no *trou*.

The Post Office

Our post office and city hall are up on National 13. I can get there by going through the little park along the *chemin de halage*. The city hall is an old chateau—in fact, it's the chateau where James II of England stayed when he was requested to leave his crown to Mary of William and Mary. The people in England felt he had the wrong religion.

The post office has been replaced and rebuilt since we came. The original was on the corner of National 13 and Jean-Jaurès. The new post office is next to the *mairie*. It's so great in France to have a post office where they know you, where they'll sell you the special collection stamps without a fuss and will make recommendations for the least expensive ways to mail a package. It's almost as good as having a dentist for a friend.

The old post office up on the corner is now a restaurant. It has a lunchtime menu for about a hundred and twenty francs, way out of our category. However, we have such a selection of fine restaurants, it isn't missed. There is a great Savoie-style restaurant near us, too. They specialize in various types of fondue, from cheese through different meat fondues. It isn't very expensive and has a graceful and quiet atmosphere.

Chapter XXII

Finale, I Hope

So, as one can easily see, all the work on the houseboat has paid off. We have a comfortable, inexpensive place to live surrounded by beauty, the river, the village, other houseboats and natural countryside. All this is within twelve miles of Paris. It's turning out to be a dream come true after all the nightmare moments trying to put it together.

It's difficult to describe a typical day for us, now that Rosemary is retired and I'm flirting with it. It's very dependent on the weather, especially in the winter with the floods.

The river rises uncomfortably about one winter in three. Most times the first floods are just after Christmas and sometimes last until the end of April. The winter weather can be quite cold, usually about five degrees Celsius colder than the weather in Paris. So, heating is a major problem for us. We sometimes also have ice on the river, thin layers of windblown ice sliding over each other with a swishing sound and packing around the hull of the boat as if to freeze it in place. But, oddly enough, it isn't humid, only cold. I think it's the winds blowing along the river, blowing away the mists.

Heating the boat can be a big problem. The cost of electricity in France is high, and our prime heating has been with electric, oil-filled radiators. We've also used butane catalytic space heaters, but it's a nuisance driving into Bougival to replace the gas bottles every two weeks or so.

We've made some interesting arrangements with EDF, Électricité de France. First, because there is less domestic use of electric power after eleven o'clock in the evening and before six o'clock in the morning, they encourage the installation of a separate meter, called a *compteur bleu,* for night usage. It allows for half price on electric power used during those hours. This means we run our washer or dryer, dishwasher, heaters—anything pulling brute electricity—only during the night.

Then, because of the heavy winter drain on the need for power, the EDF will make another deal with the consumer. If, during the twenty-one coldest days in the year, we are willing to pay *ten* times the usual day rate, all other electricity used will be at the night rate, whether used day or night. We signed up for this system called *un jour de point.* The EDF decides which twenty-one days will be expensive. We've installed, at their suggestion, and our expense, a signal light that tells us by ten o'clock in the evening when the next day will be one of these high-price days. Those days, we use no electricity except reading lights and the refrigerator, and it's so cold the refrigerator hardly runs at all. We run our Franklin open wood stove and a few butane heaters full blast during these days.

In winter, our usual life pattern is something like this. We do not heat the boat at all during the night. With all that Styrofoam I've installed, in the walls, floors, ceiling, even under the rugs, the boat is almost like an ice cream box.

I wake naturally at six in the morning. It gets to be *more* naturally as I grow older. Forces of nature. I go peek at the indicator to see if this is one of the high-price days. If not, I come back to the living room, turn on all the heaters, turn on some jazz, then do my yoga and calisthenics. By eight o'clock the boat is warm. I've laid out breakfast dishes, gone to the bakery for bread, and Rosemary has taken her shower. While she fixes breakfast, I luxuriate in my shower. I'm usually pretty sweaty from the workout. Then we have breakfast together. At nine, I bundle up and go to the post office to pick up mail and send out our own mail. Sometimes the boat is up with the flood and my trip down the icy, slanted gangplank is a challenge, but nothing too frightening.

After this, Rosemary and I share the newspaper, the *International Herald Tribune,* and listen to music, mostly classical. We've heated up our offices, so by ten we go to work. I'm down at the big desk in the metal hull, Rosemary is in her ex-aviary. She's my bird in a gilded cage.

At eleven-thirty, weather permitting, and we go out in most weather, we go for our daily walk, usually about five miles. Most times we drive to one of the nearby parks, or forests, in Marly-le-Roi, St.-Germain-en-Laye, Maisons-Lafitte, or even the park of Saint-Cloud, which is near the school where Rosemary worked for so many years. We try to stop at the library of the school so Rosemary can find new books to read. She's sort of emeritus to the library.

At home, we lunch lightly, chat, read for an hour or so, then, by two-thirty, it's back to work. I have my wristwatch alarm set for five o'clock, and that's the famous five o'clock whistle. I shut down my computer, or finish the final touches on a painting, or at least find a good place to stop.

Also, during the workday down in my office, I regulate myself by a wall clock I have hanging over my desk. It's a windup clock, a seven-day clock, with Westminster chimes. It gongs on the quarter hour each time. I take a big stretch, take a deep breath, sometimes even stand to loosen my back and neck muscles, while looking out at the river flow by. I go back to work refreshed.

It's now before dinner when we often take a walk along the

chemin de halage, looking at the river and the other boats, in the winter feeding the seagulls, in the spring, summer or fall, feeding the fish, ducks, geese, loons, coots or any other wildlife that camps on our bank. Rosemary says it's most pleasant and unique having a barnyard just outside the window of one's boat. We have bird feeders and also feed the ends of our daily baguette to the geese and ducks. Recently, we've been having visitations by blue herons. We started with one and are now up to three. They have a difficult time finding places where they can live and breed. Apparently they've found a place on our *bras mort* of the Seine. We're looking forward to having baby herons visit. We don't feed them; they live by catching fish in the shallows near the bank.

We have fun cooking, nothing extraordinary, or too much work, things we enjoy and can afford. We usually dine by candlelight with the Franklin stove fire burning. It's one of those more modern versions with doors, so it's like an open fireplace. After dinner and kitchen cleanup, there's more listening to music and reading time, or, once in a while, a friend will stop by, or we'll phone our children or friends with whom we keep in contact. It's a very quiet and peaceful existence.

The exception is the boat itself. A houseboat, like housework, is never done. There's the usual maintenance one would expect, such as repairs to damage done by flooding, replacement of broken boards, much painting, varnishing the wood of the upper boat, and, every other year, a scraping of the hull and repainting of the lower metal hull. It's also the time we clean windows down there. I'm in the dinghy outside maneuvering by ropes hanging from the deck, washing away. I need to pull myself back after each good rub on the window; the old physical rule of "for every action there is an equal and opposite reaction" can be a pain in the neck when washing windows in a small boat. It's the same problem with the painting of the hull. Rosemary goes along on the inside of the windows, catching the spots I miss and cleaning her side. It's good sunny-weather work.

I still can't believe how user-friendly this boat is now, after all the blood and sweat I, Sam, Matt, Tom, M. Teurnier and Gaston had putting it together. If one squints, one can't even tell it's two boats anymore. At least I can't. They look as if they've been married all their lives.

Speaking of marriages, Rosemary and I have been married forty-six years now. We look forward to celebrating our golden anniversary on this boat with our friends and children. It will bring back so many memories of good times had.

Each of the seasons has its beauty. In spring there are the candle blossoms of chestnuts all along the riverbanks, then their snowlike dropping of the petals when the wind blows. There's the growing of a ground cover by wild cucumber, the yellow blossoming of the willows overhanging the boat and the quick, sharp smells of the maples as they leaf out.

For the last few years we've had little tits, called *mésanges,* literally translated "my angels," who build their nest in a birdhouse I've constructed and hung on the side of the wooden boat. We watch them from the gathering of the nesting materials through the first peepings, the wild gathering of insects to satisfy the young as they grow and then the almost mysterious, instantaneous departure from the nest, as if on a signal. For a few weeks we watch the young clumsily chasing their parents through the trees to be fed one last "beakful."

Also, in spring there is the hatching of wild ducklings. This year the mother duck built her nest in a cranny on our upper deck, and we watched as she encouraged each of the thirteen in her brood to make the big jump into the river. They're mallard ducks, wild and free.

Fall is beautiful in its own way, the turning of the leaves, the speeding up of the river with the fresh rains, the frantic restlessness of the songbirds as they gather for their flight to warmer weather in the south. The first arrival of the seagulls who've hitched rides inland on the barges that pass on the other side of the island and stayed for the winter. The leaves fall into the river and float like small boats with the current.

And now winter again. Rosemary wants me to install central heating. I've figured how I can do it by using the front ballast tanks for storing the oil and having gravity feed to the heater. I could install two radiators in the downstairs and two in the upstairs using flexible copper tubing and olive joints for the plumbing. But I can see already that I'm not going to do it this year. There must be an end somewhere to the demands of this boat.

But I know I'll do it sooner or later. When I'm older, I might not be so eager to jump out of bed at six o'clock of a morning in the bitter cold. We'll wait and see.

So, finally I end this saga of a boat, of a good part of our lives, our private saga. I can't imagine what we'd be like now if this boat hadn't happened to our family, but I'm sure our friend Jo Lancaster was right. We're all better for it, not just in the comforts and joys of the present, but with the knowledge that, even without many skills, we did it. Our boat floats!

About the Author

WILLIAM WHARTON is the pseudonym for the author of eight novels: *Birdy, Dad, A Midnight Clear, Scumbler, Pride, Tidings, Franky Furbo,* and *Last Lovers.* He has also written the memoir *Ever After. Birdy* won the American Book Award for best first novel when it was published in 1978, became a national bestseller, and was made into an award-winning film. *Dad* was a National Book Award nominee. A native of Philadelphia, Wharton fought in World War II, where he was part of the Army Specialized Training Program. In 1960, he received a Ph.D. in psychology from UCLA and moved to France. There Wharton made his living as a painter while raising his two daughters and two sons. The tragic death of his daughter Kate, her husband, and two infant daughters was the subject of *Ever After.* He now lives with his wife, Rosemary, outside of Paris on a houseboat on the Seine.